Electoral Structure and Urban Policy

Bureaucracies, Public Administration, and Public Policy

Kenneth J. Meier
Series Editor

Bureaucracies, Public Administration, and Public Policy

Electoral Structure and Urban Policy

The Impact on Mexican American Communities

J. L. POLINARD
ROBERT D. WRINKLE
TOMAS LONGORIA
NORMAN E. BINDER

Routledge
Taylor & Francis Group
LONDON AND NEW YORK

First published 1994 by M.E. Sharpe

Published 2015 by Routledge
2 Park Square, Milton Park, Abingdon, Oxon OX14 4RN
711 Third Avenue, New York, NY 10017, USA

Routledge is an imprint of the Taylor & Francis Group, an informa business

Library of Congress Cataloging-in-Publication Data

Electoral structure and urban policy : the impact on Mexican American
communities / J.L. Polinard . . . [et al.].
p.   cm.   — (Bureaucracies, public administration, and
public policy)
Includes bibliographical references (p.   ) and index.
ISBN 1-56324-348-2. — ISBN 1-56324-349-0 (pbk.)
1. Local elections—Texas. 2. School elections—Texas.
3. Representative government and representation—Texas.
4. Mexican Americans—Texas—Politics and government.
I. Polinard, Jerry L.
II. Series.
JS451.T45E44   1994   94-17978
324.9764—dc20
CIP

ISBN 13: 9781563243493 (pbk)
ISBN 13: 9781563243486 (hbk)

Contents

List of Tables and Figures

Figures

Foreword

The M. E. Sharpe series "Bureaucracies, Public Administration, and Public Policy" is designed as a forum for the best work on bureaucracy and its role in public policy and governance. Although the series is open with regard to approach, methods, and perspectives, especially sought are three types of research. First, the series hopes to attract theoretically informed, empirical studies of bureaucracy. Public administration has long been viewed as a theoretical and methodological backwater of political science. This view persists despite a recent accumulation of first-rate research. The series seeks to place public administration at the forefront of empirical analysis within political science. Second, the series is interested in conceptual work that attempts to clarify theoretical issues, set an agenda for research, or provide a focus for professional debates. Third, the series seeks manuscripts that challenge the conventional wisdom about how bureaucracies influence public policy or the role of public administration in governance.

Electoral Structure and Urban Policy: The Impact on Mexican American Communities falls into the third category. It examines the impact of the Voting Rights Act on Latino politics in Texas. Too many studies of minority politics and voting have been content to look at the impact of single-member districts on either city councils or school boards. This study is an attempt to provide a comprehensive analysis of the Voting Rights Act by examining electoral structures, representation on both city councils and school boards, and representation in the bureaucracy; by assessing the types of persons selected as political representatives; and by discussing what difference it all makes. By combining the rich detail of case studies with rigorous quantitative analysis, the authors have provided a view of the political and policy changes that occur when electoral structures are changed.

Electoral Structure and Urban Policy is also a contribution to the literature on minority politics. Latinos now play a key role in the politics of Texas, California, Florida, New York, and numerous other states; they have become an important electoral group nationally because they reside in states that possess clout in the electoral college. By providing a wide-angle view of Latino politics in Texas, the authors reveal the smaller political struggles that have contributed to making Latinos a political force in the United States. By building political organizations and gaining political success at the local level, Latinos have constructed a base for forays into national politics. *Electoral Structure and Urban Policy* is must reading for scholars and students seeking to understand Latino politics, Texas politics, and the full impact of the Voting Rights Act on the civil rights of U.S. citizens.

Kenneth J. Meier

Preface and Acknowledgments

This book is a result of the authors' varied interests in the study of electoral reform, minority politics, and urban policy. Several features came together to help focus the research. The Voting Rights Act (VRA) provided a contemporary legal weapon in the quest for equity for minorities in our political system. Several important works by noted scholars, including Heilig and Mundt's *Your Voice at City Hall*, Browning, Marshall, and Tabb's *Protest Is Not Enough*, and Welch and Bledsoe's *Urban Reform and Its Consequences*, stimulated and guided our interest. Meier and England's early *APSR* article and their subsequent work with Joe Stewart on *Race, Class and Education: The Politics of Second Generation Discrimination* and then Meier and Stewart's *Politics of Hispanic Education* provided an impetus to expand our focus to school boards as well as city councils. Our intellectual debt to these scholars is quite large.

We decided to focus our work on one state for several reasons. First, it allowed us to concentrate on one Latino minority group—Mexican Americans. Second, by concentrating on a single state, we were able to enrich our quantitative analysis with some case study work over a period of years. Third, Texas is an appropriate research choice, given its racial and ethnic diversity and long history of objections under the VRA. In addition to those reasons, it afforded us an excellent and varied selection of towns, cities, and school districts for our analysis.

Of course, equal access to the councils of government is an ongoing process. Our analysis of the impact of electoral reform in cities and schools, with an emphasis on policy outputs, extends our knowledge of this process.

Our research could not have been possible without substantial support from a number of sources. Partial support was given by a grant from the Inter-University Program for Latino Research funded by the Ford Foundation. Additional support was provided by grants from the Faculty Research Council at the University of Texas–Pan American and from the University of Texas at Brownsville. We gratefully acknowledge all support.

Part of chapter 6 is derived from J. L. Polinard, Tomas Longoria, and Robert D. Wrinkle, "The Impact of District Elections on the Mexican American Community: The Electoral Perspective," *Social Science Quarterly* 72 (September 1991): 608–614, by permission of *Social Science Quarterly* and the University of Texas Press.

Also, part of chapter 6 is derived from Robert D. Wrinkle, Tomas Longoria, J. L. Polinard, and Kenneth J. Meier, "Mexican Americans and Municipal Employment: The Impact of Status and Pay Levels," *State and Local Government Review* 24 (Winter 1992): 36–42, by permission of *State and Local Government Review*, published by Carl Vinson Institute, University of Georgia.

Another part of chapter 6 is taken, in part, from J. L. Polinard, Robert D. Wrinkle, and Tomas Longoria, "Representation and Policy: Appointments of Mexican Americans to Boards and Commissions," *Social Science Journal* 28 (April 1991): 259–66, by permission of *Social Science Journal*.

Part of chapter 7 is based on J. L. Polinard, Robert D. Wrinkle, and Tomas Longoria, "Education and Governance: Representational Links to Second Generation Discrimination," *Western Political Quarterly* (September 1990): 631–46, by permission of *Political Research Quarterly* and the University of Utah.

We would also like to thank our colleagues Charles Cotrell, Rodolfo de la Garza, Bernard Grofman, Ken Meier, Joe Stewart, and Susan Welch for their assistance, above and beyond the call of duty, in sharing questionnaires, data, and ideas. Their help was vital to our research. Meier, as editor of the M. E. Sharpe book series and as a colleague, was tireless in his support and encouragement. Michael Weber and his staff at M. E. Sharpe provided encouragement and assistance. We would also like to thank the anonymous reviewers who read parts of our research as journal reviewers. Any remaining faults are, of course, ours alone.

Electoral
Structure
and
Urban Policy

1

Introduction

It could even develop into a minor revolution of sorts.
Those people up there have traditionally had long fuses,
but they do have fuses. . . . Still, most of those people are
scared stiff of authority. . . . Yet they are also curious right
now. . . . I'll tell you frankly, I don't want to misjudge [the]
capacity for drawing those people together and causing
trouble. . . . Maybe it doesn't seem so now, but that's poten-
tially one hell of a volatile area up there.

John Nichols,
The Milagro Beanfield War

For the past twenty-five years, a "minor revolution of sorts" has occurred throughout the South and Southwest as local governments have
altered their electoral structures in response to voting rights litigation
or the threat thereof. Implicit in these activities is the belief in a link
between electoral structure and the nature of representation. Our research joins the exploration of this relationship. Essentially, we ask
whether it makes a difference to the minority population of a community if city council or school board members are elected at-large or by
geographically defined districts.

American democracy ultimately is an experiment. Americans take
the notion that the people have the right to govern themselves, and we
tinker and fuss with the subtle and not-so-subtle complexities of how
best to do so. We began as a people, two hundred years ago, with the
rather radical idea that "all men are created equal," defining the reference to gender literally and redefining the inclusive "all" to "some" so
as to exclude the nonwhite and the nonwealthy. Then, for two centuries,

3

we engaged in an experiment of expanding the idea of self-government to embrace the diverse sectors of our polity.

We Americans assert that, in the political philosophy of our system, there is a certain nobility to this experiment. At the same time, there is also the pragmatism of the distribution of political power, for the issue of who represents whom has direct policy consequences. It is an interesting wedding of philosophy and practice, this tension between democracy (with its majoritarian impulse) and representation (which recognizes numerical strength as just one index of merit).

Initially, attempts to resolve that tension extended the franchise through constitutional amendments and court decisions. The 1960s brought the reapportionment revolution and the application of the one-person, one-vote rule to virtually all levels of American politics. In 1965 the passage of the Voting Rights Act (VRA) heralded an emphasis on voter registration and access to the polls for racial and ethnic minorities. The VRA was designed to ensure equity for minorities in terms of access to the political system.

Subsequent amendments to the VRA have shifted its focus to the structures of local electoral systems. The result has been a revolution with consequences potentially as profound as those produced by the implementation of the one-person, one-vote principle during the 1960s and 1970s. Throughout the South and Southwest, the VRA has been used to change local election systems from at-large to district or mixed structures. In the main, those changes have been initiated, and welcomed, by the minority populations, but in the 1990s voices have been heard suggesting that such changes have brought mixed blessings.[1]

One of the most enduring of all political axioms is that no one in power relinquishes it voluntarily. This axiom is validated when one examines the historical political relationship between Anglo and Latino communities in the United States. Whether one looks at the national, state, or local community, the same pattern emerges: Anglos historically control the political processes of the community, and any transition of power from the Anglo to the Latino community occurs as a result of aggressive efforts on the part of the Latino community, which are strongly resisted by the Anglo community.

Our inquiry in this work focuses on this transition of power. How does the Latino community organize, mobilize, develop, and execute strategies that result in increased political influence over, and in some cases control of, the political processes of the local community? In other words, we seek to understand the variables that lead to the assumption of power where powerlessness existed before.

Approaches to Minority Politics

Minority politics has long been a staple of political science research. Much of the early work focused on white European ethnics within the scope of national politics (Wolfinger 1965). Restrictive immigration policies and the growth of the existing minority populations have shifted that focus to persons of color in American society (Bass and DeVries 1976; Matthews and Prothro 1966). While much of the focus of minority politics has been on the black community, the emergence of the Latinos as a significant force in American society also has attracted scholarly attention (de la Garza 1984; Grebler, Moore, and Guzman 1970).

One approach to studying minority representation most often addresses the issue in terms of proportionality. That is, minorities are considered underrepresented or overrepresented on the basis of the proportion of offices they hold compared with their proportion of the population (see Cayer and Sigelman 1980; Dye and Renick 1981; Eisinger 1982; Engstrom and McDonald 1981, 1982; Grofman 1982; Heilig and Mundt 1984; Jones 1976; Karnig 1976; Karnig and Welch 1980; Lineberry 1978; MacManus 1978; Robinson and Dye 1978; Robinson and England 1981).

The focus on proportionality leans heavily on what Pitkin calls "descriptive representation"—that is, representation defined in terms of the characteristics of the representatives—and "passive representation," in which the emphasis is on "being something rather than doing something" (Pitkin 1967, 67). This contrasts with active representation, where the representative engages in activity on behalf of the represented. Much research on minority representation has concentrated on descriptive representation (Meier and England 1984; Robinson, England, and Meier 1985).

The literature on electoral systems and passive representation essentially confirms what Davidson and Korbel term the "conventional hypothesis" (1981, 92–93): that at-large election systems dilute minority representation (for summaries, see also Heilig and Mundt 1984; Meier and England 1984; Polinard, Wrinkle, and Longoria 1990, 1991). These examinations of how minority representation evolves traditionally use broad national studies based on samples of cities, generally those with over 50,000 in population (Bullock and MacManus 1990; Engstrom and McDonald 1986; Welch 1990).

The other major approach to studying minority politics has examined the effects of urban structure on the minority population. Much of this research uses case study designs and has developed a wealth of material that has enriched our knowledge concerning urban politics in general and minority politics in particular. One of the major findings from this research is that minority representation within the dominant governing coalition on city councils leads to policies favorable to minority groups (Browning, Marshall, and Tabb 1984).

Despite the contributions of these research efforts to our knowledge of minority representation, descriptive representation studies tell us little about representation as an activity. The link between passive and active representation with respect to minority communities has received little attention. (For exceptions, see Dye and Renick 1981; Eisinger 1982; Fraga, Meier, and England 1986; Heilig and Mundt 1984; and Meier and England 1984.) This is a significant area of inquiry and any complete understanding of the relationship between electoral structure and minority representation cannot ignore this link. We need to know not only if electoral structure facilitates or obstructs the election of minority candidates, but also if the election of minority candidates translates into active representation through policy benefits for the minority community.

This book blends the quantitative cross-sectional approach with the case study approach in order to develop more fully our understanding of the impact of the issues of structure, representation, and outcomes on a minority community. By the combination of these approaches, our analyses should be enhanced.

Election Structures in Urban Politics Research

There are two distinct literatures on the impact of urban institutional structures. Early studies of "reformism" structures, such as council-manager government, at-large elections, and civil service, examined the changes that occurred at the end of the nineteenth century and during the early years of the twentieth century. Those changes were motivated by the desire of local "good government" civic groups to break up urban political machines, thereby limiting the power of emerging immigrant groups. Despite this intent, empirical research did not find significant fiscal policy differences between reformed and unreformed cities (see, e.g., Liebert 1974; Lineberry and Fowler 1967; Morgan and Pelissero 1980; Wolfinger and Field 1966).

Studies of contemporary urban institutional reform—primarily changing election structures from at-large to single-member districts—examine changes beginning in the early 1970s and continuing today. Such changes result from demands for equal representation by minority groups and are facilitated by the federal government through the VRA. Empirical research, in general, finds that there is greater representational equity under single-member district election systems (Davidson and Korbel 1981; Engstrom and McDonald 1981; MacManus 1978; Polinard, Wrinkle, and Longoria 1991). Others find that city size, not election structure, is related to representational equity (Taebel 1978). In a recent paper, Bullock and MacManus (1993, 295) consider several features of the "totality of circumstances" test and find that "blacks are more likely to be elected in cities that have larger councils and in which there was greater turnover in the most recent election." They also find (1993, 296) that blacks are disadvantaged by certain forms of at-large elections and that the impact of election structures has diminished over time (see also Welch 1990).

Most discussion of representational equity generally has been in terms of descriptive representation. Descriptive representation, while important, usually does not address the issue of what policy consequences for the minority community exist when representation is enhanced. Exceptions to this are studies that have linked district elections structures to more equitable minority employment patterns in cities (Mladenka 1989a) and less discriminatory education policy in schools (Meier and Stewart 1991). These studies are part of a new wave of research focused on institutional structure and policy impact. Findings from the literature that show that institutional structure and representation affect policy challenge research that argues that cities are constrained and have a limited ability to affect local policy and make a difference in the lives of city residents (Peterson 1981).

The finding that structure and representation matter suggests that election structure and minority representation should play a central role in the study of urban governance. However, this is not the case. Before the structure and representation literature can be fully integrated into urban research and theory, research on urban minority representation and policy first must be reconciled with Peterson's assertion that local governments are inherently limited in what they can do to satisfy local demands. One reason for the lack of theoretical stock placed in the issue of election structure is that many urban scholars reject the view of cities as "independent policy-producing units," where local government officials have a considerable amount of substantive policy-making discretion (see Peterson 1981). This view holds that cities lack resources and authority to affect their own well-being. As a consequence, urban politics research is dominated by the study of economic conditions and political economy (Vogel 1992), rather than by study of the impact of municipal structures and representation.

Several urban politics researchers challenge Peterson's model of urban policy making, arguing that cities do, in fact, have policy discretion (see the exchange between Stone and Sanders 1987; see also Browning, Marshall, and Tabb 1984; Peterson 1981; Stone 1989). The relevance of election structure and representation for urban politics research and theory is enhanced if it is linked with the models of urban governance outlined by Stone and by Browning, Marshall, and Tabb. We argue here that election structure and minority representation are directly linked to regime theory (Stone 1989) and incorporation theory (Browning, Marshall, and Tabb 1984).

Stone argues forcefully that urban regimes—informal relationships between the citizens, government, and the business sectors of society —are more important than formal institutions and structure. Urban regimes create and build a governing capacity that enables government to enhance its power and to address its problems more effectively (Stone 1989). Browning, Marshall, and Tabb emphasize political incorporation in which bargaining and coalition building are important determinants of local government policy making. Following Pitkin, researchers Browning, Marshall, and Tabb examine symbolic as well as substantive representation and conclude that unless an elected official is part of the governing coalition, representation can be only symbolic. We believe institutional structures play a larger role in those theories than either Stone or Browning et al. acknowledge.

There is conceptual overlap between Browning, Marshall, and Tabb's political incorporation concept, Stone's regime politics concept, and the role of election structures for minority representation. Browning, Marshall, and Tabb (1984) argue that political incorporation leads to substantive policy consequences. The level of political incorporation increases when minority council members are elected, when minority council members become part of the dominant governing coalition, and when a member of a minority group controls the mayoralty (1984, 272). In two of ten cities they examined, the election of minority council members occurred only after district election structures had been adopted (1984, 202). In five of the ten cities, district elections increased the number of minority council members (Browning, Marshall, and Tabb 1984, 202). Since they do not control for the form of elections because of a "lack of variance" (1984, 84), political incorporation may be spurious with the changes in election structure.

Stone (1989, 81) argues that Atlanta's governing regime went through a restructuring partly as a consequence of the election of Mayor Maynard Jackson in 1973, when there was "a stark reversal of the political past" of an elite-dominated city council. A new city charter, approved in 1973, changed the election structure from at-large to a mixed, or hybrid, system; mobilized Atlanta's neighborhood organizations; increased black political participation; and paved the way for Mayor Jackson's election (1989, 84). Like the congruence between structural change and political incorporation, in the case of Stone's regime framework the linkage between structural change and regime change is clear, but not considered.

Political Resources Model

In addition to the political incorporation model and the regime politics model, which rely primarily on case studies, the political resources model is used to examine urban politics and policy consequences for minority groups. The political resources model is closely linked to resource mobilization theory derived from sociology (see Button 1989; Gamson 1990; McCarthy and Zald 1973), and mobilization theory from political science (Morrison 1987). Button argues that resource mobilization theory offers the best opportunity to analyze such political-social movements as the civil rights movement. Morrison (1987, 3) defines mobilization as the collective activation and application of community or group resources toward the acquisition of social and political goods. Generally it is assumed that it is the level of resources available to minorities and other out-groups that allows the development of strategies and tactics to achieve goals (see Button 1989, 14).

Morrison (1987, 8) suggests that this process occurs through a series of sequential stages:

a) the existence of values and goals requiring mobilization;
b) action on the part of leaders, elites or institutions seeking to mobilize individuals and groups;
c) the institutional and collective means of achieving this mobilization;
d) the symbols and references by which values, goals and norms are communicated to, and understood as internalized by, the individuals involved in mobilization.

Researchers interested in the acquisition of power by minority groups find that this approach offers an opportunity to study the structural and policy implications of such a transfer of power.

The political resources model used in most aggregate research studies consists primarily of demographic variables that serve as surrogate variables for political resources. For example, the percentage of population that is minority, the white/black income ratio, and the level of education are all used to measure the ability of minority groups to press demands on local government (Meier and Stewart 1989). Several important national studies focusing on minority groups in urban politics have used this model (Welch 1990; Meier and Stewart 1991).

Enhanced Political Resources Model

Existing political resources models have a number of methodological problems as applied to the national, regional, state, and local levels. Problems with national studies include (1) lack of explanation of how resources are translated into political gains (the notable exception being the studies by Meier and Stewart); (2) a focus on only larger cities; (3) potentially confounding effects, such as considering all Hispanic groups together—for example, Mexican Americans, Puerto Ricans, and Cubans—when there is evidence that the experiences of those three groups are very different; (4) failure to recognize that states may differ considerably, complicating analysis in national studies (the Welch 1990 study explicitly recognizes this and controls for it); (5) omission of theoretically important variables such as residential segregation of minority groups (Vedlitz and Johnson 1982 is an exception); and (6) emphasis on aggregate data analysis that precludes inclusion of potentially interesting contextual variables as conflict associated with the adoption of district elections.

Our study enhances the existing political resources model in a number of ways. We examine one state, to eliminate problems with intraregional and ethnic group differences. Both Button (1989) and Welch (1990) have noted the importance of region and ethnic groups. Welch (1990, 1071) has noted the need to be cautious in generalizing from the studies of large cities to smaller jurisdictions. We examine smaller cities as well as larger cities. Our aggregate analyses include all Texas cities over 20,000 population and a one-in-four sample of cities between 2,500 and 20,000 population. We include measures of residential segregation in our aggregate analysis. No previous study has done this. Our methodology includes not only aggregate data analysis but also case studies and personal interviews. Finally, because we believe that the VRA has played an important role in translating potential political resources into political representation, we include the impact of litigation as a variable in the model. Our expanded political resources model builds upon the work of Meier, Stewart, and England (1989), Meier and Stewart (1991), and Welch (1990). Our variables represent four basic forces that affect policy outputs for the Mexican American community: political resources, urban political structure, social class, and context.

Political Resources

Conventional wisdom holds that for minorities to win elections and influence public policy, they must have sufficient resources that can be converted into success at the ballot (Button 1989; Meier, Stewart, and England 1989) One significant resource is the size of the minority electorate. Minority success may not be a strictly linear relationship with the population size and percentage, but it clearly is an important factor (Keech 1968). In our analyses, we include the 1990 city population and the percentage of Mexican Americans in the population.

Electoral Structure

Urban electoral structures in this country have been greatly influenced by the urban reform movement (Banfield and Wilson 1963). One of the significant features of the urban reform movement was the replacement of the ward or district system with citywide "at-large" elections. The idea, of course, was that ward or district elections contributed to urban corruption and that cities could best be served by a more neutral structure in which representatives could vote for the interest of the city as a whole, rather than the narrow interest of a ward or district. Today, the conventional wisdom is that at-large elections "dilute" minority representation (Davidson and Korbel 1981). A recent work by Welch suggests that while "First, the ability of at-large systems to represent blacks has improved dramatically . . . at-large systems still do not provide representation quite as equitably as district systems" (1990, 1072). Urban electoral structures remain a significant influence on minority representation. We believe this variable interacts with the population variable noted above. Given that a sociological minority is almost always a numerical minority, it is difficult to see how successful that minority could be in at-large elections because of polarized voting. If a sociological majority votes for candidates from their racial or ethnic group and a sociological minority votes for candidates from its racial or ethnic minority group, the minority will virtually always lose. A basic assumption is that minorities are more proportionally represented in pure district systems or the district parts of mixed systems because they can maximize their voting power, in effect becoming "the" majority in the district. In this study we examine districted, mixed, and at-large systems.

Social Class

Social class has long been considered a major force affecting the mobilization of minority political resources (Button 1989). Whether the result of the group competition or power thesis (see Giles and Evans 1986) or of the Morrison–Wolfinger mobilization concept (Morrison 1987; Wolfinger 1965), most models of minority politics make extensive use of the social class concept. One widely used measure of relative social class is the ratio of minority to majority income. Karnig (1976) and Engstrom and McDonald (1981) relate that the black–white income ratio of a city is positively correlated with black council representation. Meier and Stewart (1991) use Hispanic median family income to Anglo median family income in their study. We use the same measure in our study.

Contextual

The context in which political resources are mobilized often is significant (Button 1989; Vogel 1992). For a study of Mexican Americans, one of the most significant contextual factors is residential segregation. The more concentrated a minority population is within a city, the better able that population would be to elect a candidate of choice under a ward or districted system. Conversely, the more diffuse a minority population is, the more difficult it would be to draw "safe" minority districts.[2] While most minorities are, to a greater or lesser degree, segregated in American cities, there are differences. Generally, blacks are more segregated than are Mexican Americans. Lopez (1981) found that blacks were more segregated than Mexican Americans in fifty-one of fifty-eight Southwestern cities. Vedlitz and Johnson (1982) examined the impact of election methods, controlling for differing levels of black residential segregation, and found that the impact of election methods differed less for groups that are less segregated. Another major study found similar results, but without actually testing for Hispanic residential segregation (Zax 1990). Zax compared regressions of black and Hispanic council membership, and his analysis "assumes that Hispanics are less segregated" (1990, 346). In fact, no studies have closely examined the impact of residential segregation of Mexican Americans on electoral success. As Welch says, "the ability of Hispanic populations to benefit from district elections may depend upon their degree of residential segregation . . . their population proportion and the state or region in which they are located" (1990, 1072). The ability of the minority population actually to use their numbers may be related to the degree of residential segregation. Thus, we include this as a major aspect of the contextual forces. In addition, we control for interregional and interstate contextual differences by focusing on one state.

Another contextual force is the size of the governing body. The size of the city council or school board may be a major limiting factor on minority success. For example, if the council has only five seats, then even a proportional scheme would require a 20 percent share of the population. If a council has nine seats, a proportional scheme would require only an 11 percent share of the population. Clearly, in districted systems, the number of city council places available may affect success, while nondistricted systems might have a designated "minority" seat under some form of slating arrangement. In one of the few studies to examine this issue, Taebel (1978) found that the size of the city council predicted minority representation.

Actual as well as potential access to decision makers is another major contextual force. One manner of looking at this variable is the incorporation concept of Browning, Marshall, and Tabb (1984), who argue that the success of minority groups depends in large part upon the degree to which they are incorporated into the dominant coalition. We look at that issue in terms of how many minority members serve on a city council or school board. To have a co-ethnic serve in a position of power allows access in ways in which a nonminority cannot serve. Heilig and Mundt entitled their 1984 book *Your Voice at City Hall* as a clear indication that minorities benefited from access to a co-ethnic.

We are also interested in the effect, if any, of the VRA on the electoral structure. Litigation or the threat of litigation could be an important resource for minorities to mobilize. We are interested in the impact that litigation has on the drawing of the districts. Cities that voluntarily redistrict may draw districts that are not as safe for minority candidates as would be those districts drawn as a result of litigation. On the other hand, to avoid litigation, cities that voluntarily change to districts first reach agreement on the composition of the districts with the potential plaintiffs. In the latter case the districts would be essentially the same as those that had been litigated. Our anecdotal evidence supports the latter alternative. We include litigation as a variable in the model.

The Nature and Setting of the Study

The purpose of this book is to analyze minority politics in the context of urban electoral and political structures. Our goal is to examine how electoral structure, representation styles, and policy outputs coalesce to affect the Mexican American community. As noted above, most studies of minority electoral success and urban political structures have featured some methodological problems. We hope to pursue our inquiry while, at the same time, avoiding the most egregious methodological problems.

By confining our focus to one state and to one ethnic group, we hope to avoid the problems of confounding noted above. Texas is an excellent choice of a research site. It is a large and varied state with a sizable minority population. Most Hispanics in the state are of Mexican origin. Further, Texas has a large number of cities of differing sizes with significant minority populations. The state also has a storied history in terms of the VRA, having sustained more VRA objections than all other states combined.

Our analyses combine two rich research traditions: case study analysis and aggregate data analysis. We have gathered aggregate data analysis from a variety of sources, including EEO-4 reports, city records, litigation files of the Mexican American Legal Defense and Education Fund (MALDEF) and Texas Rural Legal Aid, and various city officials. In addition, in 1990, we obtained (1) data from a survey of all Texas cities with populations above 20,000 and (2) a random sample (one-in-four) of Texas cities between 2,500 and 20,000 population. We collected additional data in January and February 1991, using a two-page questionnaire mailed to city clerks. Cities that failed to respond were contacted a second time with a postcard and a second mailing of the survey instrument. A total of 132 cities responded (83 percent response rate). Our survey instrument included the usual questions concerning electoral structure, size of city council, and ethnic composition of the council (a copy of the instrument is found in appendix A). The analyses of these data are reported in chapter 3. We also conducted a mail survey of the mayors and city councilpersons of the same cities. Those instruments were mailed in Fall 1992. These data are reported in chapter 4.

We also surveyed all school boards in Texas that had changed from at-large elections to some form of districting. The survey included a control sample of school districts that had not changed their electoral structures. A total of 674 usable responses were obtained (a 64 percent response rate). Our survey instrument was modeled after Welch and Bledsoe (1988). A copy of that instrument is found in appendix B; these data are reported in chapter 5.

In addition to the above aggregate data, we selected ten cities for case study analysis. Over a period of six years, we collected data and interviewed officials in all ten cities. We believe this combination of methods provides a rich and detailed interpretation of the processes of transmittal of power in Texas cities. A brief description of the ten case study cities follows.

The Cities

Ten cities serve as a focus of our inquiry. Four (Beeville, Corpus Christi, Port Lavaca, and Victoria) are located in south Texas, three

(New Braunfels, Pleasanton, and San Antonio) are located in south-central Texas, and three (Big Spring, El Paso, and Lubbock) are located in west Texas. They range in population size from 6,000 in Pleasanton to 785,880 in San Antonio. All ten have a Mexican American population of at least 18 percent.

Table 1.1 summarizes pertinent information about the ten cities at the time of their initial changeover to district elections.

Beeville

In spite of, or perhaps because of, the significant size of the Mexican American population (57 percent) in Beeville, it has not been easy to be brown and live in Beeville, a small ranching and oil-based community in south Texas. There is a long history of racial violence in the area, with an active Ku Klux Klan (KKK) during the 1920s (the country club is located just down the road from "KKK Hill"). Mexican Americans and Anglos did not attend the same elementary schools until 1949, and, as recently as 1957, a Mexican American was chained to a post at city hall by a city police officer for failure to pay a $10 fine.

In 1973 the city changed its at-large electoral system to five wards with the mayor elected by the council. This change was seen as a way of blunting the strength of the growing Mexican American vote in the at-large elections.

In December 1976, a suit was filed by MALDEF asking for four wards plus a mayor elected at-large. During the course of that litigation it was discovered that the 1973 change had never been pre-cleared with the Justice Department. The city contended that since the change had occurred prior to the extension of the VRA to Texas in 1975, no preclearance was necessary. In June 1978, that claim was rejected by a three-judge district court. In the meantime the city had been enjoined from holding any elections under the district format until the legality of the electoral system were established. The 1973 change was then submitted to the Justice Department. In February 1979 the Justice Department sustained an objection to the 1973 ward system. The city council entered into negotiations with the plaintiffs and agreed to the current plan of four wards and a mayor elected at-large. The first elections under the new system were held in April 1979.

Racial divisiveness continues to be an issue in Beeville (see the exchange concerning racism between a Mexican American and an Anglo

Table 1.1

Case Study Cities at Time of Change to District Elections

City	1980 Population	Mexican American (%)	Former System	New System	Date of Elections	Location
Beeville	14,574	57	5 wards, mayor by council	4 wards, mayor at-large	1979	South
Big Spring	24,804	24	5 at-large	3 SMD; 3 at-large, mayor at-large	1984	West
Corpus Christi	231,999	47	6 at-large; mayor at-large	5 SMD; 3 at-large, mayor at-large	1983	South
El Paso	425,259	63	At-large, replaced by 6 SMD in 1979	6 SMD; mayor at-large in 1982	1982	West
Lubbock	173,979	19	4 at-large; mayor at-large	6 SMD; mayor at-large	1984	West
New Braunfels	22,402	34	7 at-large	4 SMD; 3 at-large, mayor by council	1983	Central
Pleasanton	6,346	42	5 at-large, mayor at-large	6 SMD; mayor at-large	1984	Central
Port Lavaca	10,911	45	6 at-large	6 SMD; mayor at-large	1984	South
San Antonio	785,880	54	9 at-large, mayor at-large	10 SMD; mayor at-large	1977	Central
Victoria	50,695	34	5 at-large	4 SMD; 2 "super districts"	1981	South

SMD = single-member district.

in the "Letters to the Editor" section of the November 25, 1992, Beeville Bee-Picayune.) This has resulted in a continuing fight over the drawing of new district lines for the city as well as virtually every other issue.

Big Spring

The atmosphere is grim in Big Spring, a small west Texas ranching and oil community (about 25,000 population) with about one-fourth of its population Mexican American. The community has been hard hit by the closing of a military base and the weakened Texas oil economy. Nonetheless, the townsfolk are spirited. That spirit may be best represented by the optimistic soul who named his Big Spring motel the "Ocean View Motel." Alas, the business folded, perhaps, in part, due to the fact that the nearest ocean to view is over five hundred miles away. Spirited townsfolk or no, Big Spring was not a particularly happy place to be in the mid-1980s.

Big Spring has never been a particularly pleasant place to be if you are Mexican American. Mexican American children attended the Negro School in the 1920s; during that period, the Mexican American teacher received a lower salary than the Anglo janitor at the Anglo school. In 1931 the school board authorized the construction of a school for "Mexicans," but ordered it closed during cotton-picking season so the schoolchildren could work in the fields. In 1944 there were five teachers for the 600 Mexican American schoolchildren. In 1976 federal funds were withheld from the school district due to the finding that the district maintained a segregated school system.

Prior to the 1980s no Mexican American had ever been elected to the city council, school board, or junior college district board. While Mexican Americans were fairly numerous and were somewhat organized (there was a chapter of the League of United Latin American Citizens [LULAC]), they were not mobilized effectively. In fact, when there was talk of entering into litigation to force the city to change its electoral system, the original LULAC chapter was unwilling to do so. An alternative chapter (#4375) was formed. In November 1982, three members of the newly organized LULAC chapter, assisted by the Southwest Voter Registration Education Project, filed suit against the city's at-large election scheme. Following negotiations between the city and the plaintiffs, the city agreed in September 1983 to change its at-large system to a hybrid plan containing three single-member districts, three at-large seats, and a mayor elected at-large. The first elections under this system were held in April 1984 and resulted in the first Mexican American to hold elective city office.

Because of the original court order, and the 1990 census, the re-drawing of district lines became an issue early in 1991. Again, there was the threat of litigation if the city did not agree to a new set of districts. After negotiations between the city and the potential litigants, a new agreement was reached. The new agreement calls for six single-member districts and a mayor elected at-large. There is no residential requirement. The districts will have two minority districts with minority populations under 55 percent. Before agreement, Rolando Rios, who had represented the plaintiffs in the original suit, suggested that cumulative voting be considered. The city council was adamantly opposed. The 1993 elections were the first held under the new system. The three at-large seats were up for election. The other incumbents will serve out their terms.

Corpus Christi

Corpus Christi is the "sparkling city by the sea," one of the most attractive cities in Texas. Its origin dates from its discovery by Europeans in 1519, and it was incorporated as a town in 1849. Corpus Christi has long based its wealth and community health on its natural surroundings, a large, sheltered bay, and ample natural resources in the nearby countryside. As the *Corpus Christi Caller Times* put it,

> Corpus Christi achieved its modern economic importance almost overnight, an importance based largely upon surrounding natural wealth—chiefly that of agriculture and petroleum—and upon the shipping of its exports through a deep water port. (1951, 11)

There is less sparkle to the "sparkling city," however, on the west side of town where the Mexican American population is concentrated. In the 1950s the city's ethnic and racial neighborhoods were sufficiently contiguous that a popular joke held that the ethnic high school's (there were only two high schools at the time: one predominantly Anglo; the other, ethnically mixed) football team called its signals: "Uno, dos, tres, fo', hut!"

No Mexican Americans served on the city council from 1909 until 1955. Beginning in 1955, Mexican Americans began to show some electoral success. From 1955 through 1981 nine Mexican Americans were elected to the city council, although only one came from the west side (*Alonzo et al.* v. *Jones,* 1983). In 1970 the city charter was revised to change the plurality requirement for the at-large seats to a majority requirement, a move perceived as diluting the minority vote.

In December 1981, four Mexican American citizens filed suit against the electoral system. The lawsuit was the culmination of work begun by the Coastal Bend Legal Services in 1979 and was precipitated by the 1981 elections, when no Mexican American was elected to the council.

Following a four-day trial in the fall of 1982, Federal District Judge George Kazen ruled on February 3, 1983, that the current electoral system violated the VRA. The plaintiffs and the city negotiated an agreement, and elections were scheduled for August 1983. The new plan called for five districts, three at-large seats, and a mayor elected at-large.

Over the next five elections, no Mexican Americans won an at-large seat, and in 1992 the city found itself back in court defending the hybrid system, while the plaintiffs argued for all city council seats to be districted. The trial was completed in 1993, but the federal judge had not announced his decision as of April 1994.

El Paso

El Paso is unique. It sits on both the Texas–Mexico and Texas–New Mexico borders, giving the city a flavor like no other in the state. It is a distinctly Southwestern city, with a "feel" more like Albuquerque or Tucson than Houston or Dallas. The city also is large, with more than 400,000 population and about a two-thirds Mexican American majority. The border influence is pervasive, creating a tricultural environment: the Anglo American culture, the Mexican culture, and the "Tex-Mex" culture peculiar to Texas border cities. Perhaps because of this unique environment, there is less of the dark side to the relationships between Anglos and Mexican Americans in El Paso than in most of the other cities in our study.

In 1977 the city charter was amended to eliminate the at-large system and replace it with six alderman districts. The districts were drawn in such a way as to enhance Anglo voting strength. In May 1982, the city council established the Alderman Redistricting Advisory Committee to redistrict the six districts. Although 63 percent of the population in El Paso is Mexican American, only four of the fifteen members of the committee were Latinos.

Nonetheless, it was clear that the new districts would have to recognize the ethnic distribution of the population or El Paso would find itself in court. More than twenty organizations representing the Mexican American community spoke at the public hearings of the committee, demanding more equitably drawn districts. In spite of that testimony, the committee voted to recommend a plan that had been criticized by the Mexican American leadership. Responding to the criticisms, and no doubt with an eye toward avoiding litigation, the city council rejected the committee's recommendation and adopted an alternative plan that had the support of the Mexican American organizations. The new plan, which called for six single-member districts and an at-large mayor, was adopted in Fall 1982. In the elections of the 1980s, there was a slight increase in Mexican American candidates, but approximately the same percentage of Mexican American winners.

Following the 1990 census, new districts were created: there would be eight districts for the 1993 elections. The new districts were approved by the U.S. Department of Justice. Of the eight, four have Latino majorities. Theoretically, the districts could have been drawn in such a way as to have eight Latino majority districts, but this could not be done without unseating incumbents, and the districting committee chose not to do it.

Lubbock

Lubbock is one of the larger cities in the study, with a population of more than 170,000, almost 20 percent Mexican American. It is the quintessential west Texas town. Hot in the summer, cold in the winter, a tornado here, a dust storm there, it is a great place to live if one has a fear of mountains. Still, Lubbock residents manifest a fierce loyalty to their city; it is a community of no small civic pride. This pride, however, has a distinctly Anglo tint.

In the first quarter of the twentieth century, Lubbock was the scene of KKK activities, a legacy that continued into the middle of the century. In the late 1960s and early 1970s, some strikes by garbage workers (97 percent of whom were Mexican Americans) resulted in the city posting police officers with police dogs at some of the city council meetings. By the early 1970s only eighteen Mexican American graduates of the Lubbock school system had received a college degree.

Prior to the 1980s no Mexican American had ever been elected to the city council, and only one had run prior to 1970. Litigation challenging the city's at-large system began in 1976. In 1979 a federal district court found for the city, but the Fifth Circuit remanded the case in 1982 in light of recent Supreme Court decisions. In March 1984, the district court reversed itself and found for the plaintiffs, ordering a new electoral plan to be adopted. The Fifth Circuit upheld the order in March 1984. The new structure included six council members elected from districts and a mayor elected at-large.

The Lubbock case was one of the most expensive of the redistricting suits in Texas and cost the city several thousand dollars in legal fees. This had a direct impact on other Texas cities, many of which chose to negotiate when confronted by the threat of VRA litigation rather than face the same fate that had befallen Lubbock.

New Braunfels

This predominantly German community sits on the edge of the beautiful Texas hill country. It is fairly small (under 25,000 population). Historically, Mexican Americans, who constitute almost a quarter of the city's population, have had little political or social clout. From 1928 to 1983 only six of the seventeen Mexican Americans who ran for the 217 contested school board seats won. In the early part of the century some stores and theaters in New Braunfels were off-limits to Mexican Americans. In 1953, Henry B. Gonzales, then newly elected to the San Antonio city council, drove his family to New Braunfels to picnic in one of the city's lovely parks. The future member of the U.S. House of Representatives was asked to leave; Mexican Americans were not allowed in the park.

Following prodding from MALDEF, New Braunfels changed its election system in April 1983, from seven at-large seats to four single-member districts and three at-large places. Elections were held in August 1983, and the first Mexican American since 1973 was elected. In September 1983, MALDEF assisted in a court suit filed ostensibly to eliminate the at-large seats, but in reality to force the city council to remove the place requirements from the at-large offices. That it agreed to do and the suit was dropped.

Following the 1990 census, the council redistricted without any controversy, although the districts were not drawn in such a way as to enhance Mexican American representation.

Pleasanton

Things were not very pleasant in Pleasanton during the redistricting conflicts in the 1980s. Pleasanton is a small (6,300 population) community with a sizable (42 percent) Mexican American population, located in Atasoca County, just southwest of San Antonio. As one longtime resident noted, "If apathy was a social disease, Pleasanton would be quarantined." Actually, given the conflict that marked Pleasanton's politics during the early 1980s, apathy would be a welcome relief.

For example, the minutes of the April 18, 1983 city council meeting (taken verbatim [!] due to the divisions on the council) show the following exchanges:

Council member A: I . . . recommend that the council instruct the city manager to terminate immediately the Chief of Police.

Council member B: I'll second [the motion].

City manager: I have seen no written allegations . . . therefore, I respectfully request council reconsideration . . .

Council member A: Is the city manager refusing [to fire the police chief]?

City manager: Yes, sir, I am, until such time as I get written allegations.

Council member A: Mr. Mayor, I'd like to make a motion to [fire the city manager].

Mayor: Now just a minute.

Council member A: I've made a motion.

Council member B: I'll second the motion. *[Motion passed.]*

Mayor: Since you fellows are head-hunting tonight, you got anybody else you want to chop?

Later, following subsequent elections, both the city manager and the chief of police who were fired were returned to their old positions. One of the council members who took part in the "Tuesday Night Massacre" remained on the council; for a time he was forbidden by the city manager to speak directly to the city manager and had to communicate with him through the city secretary.

Although no Mexican American had ever been elected mayor of Pleasanton, there usually was at least one Mexican American on the city council. This was classic co-optation politics. One Anglo observer told the authors, "We always felt we should have someone to represent their [Mexican American] community, and we went to great lengths to get one to run." Referring to a recent Mexican American councilperson who had also served during the predistricting period, the same observer said, "[He] had always voted right; he didn't cause any trouble until he got some help."

"Help" arrived in the fall of 1983, when a group of Mexican American citizens organized the Citizens for Better Representation in Pleasanton to explore the need for changing the electoral system. At times they met in a member's place of business; to avoid detection they would turn off the lights and creep beneath the large plate-glass window that overlooked the main street. Aided by MALDEF, they filed suit in January 1984. The city negotiated and agreed to the new plan of six districted seats and a mayor elected at-large. The first elections under the new system were held in April 1984. These elections resulted in greatly increased representational equity for Pleasanton, as well as increased conflict on the council.

By the 1990s, however, Pleasanton seemed to be putting the bad times behind. With a relatively harmonious new council and a new city manager, there was little conflict over the drawing of new district lines following the 1990 census. Economically, things picked up, with a new industrial park and new companies coming to town.

Port Lavaca

Port Lavaca is one of several small (about 11,000 population), quiet communities that hug the Texas coastline along Highway 35. Almost half of its population (45 percent) is Mexican American, most of whom are concentrated in two neighborhoods located in or near the center of the city.

The city's history of racial and ethnic segregation and discrimination parallels that of many Texas communities. From 1932 to 1958 no Mexican American ran for local office. After one Mexican American ran in 1958, no other Mexican American stepped forward until 1970. No Mexican American had been elected to the school board since its inception in 1948. In 1956 the city increased the size of its city council from five members to six, all elected at-large. The mayor also was elected at-large. Following the April 1983 elections, representatives from MALDEF met with local Mexican American citizens, and a decision was made to seek to change the electoral structure. A previous attempt to alter the electoral system had failed one year earlier, when a Charter Revision Committee voted against recommending single-member districts to the city council. The vote was 3–2, with the two Mexican Americans on the committee in dissent.

A suit challenging the at-large scheme was filed in April 1983. The mayor expressed hope for a negotiated outcome, and, by the summer, the parties had agreed to a system of six districted seats plus a mayor elected at-large. The first elections were held in April 1984. Mexican Americans won council seats and greatly increased their representational equity.

San Antonio

San Antonio is one of the most charming cities in the United States, taking its place alongside New York, San Francisco, Chicago, and New Orleans as cities with their own unique ethic. San Antonio's rich history enhances its bicultural nature. Over half the population is Mexican American, and the city was led for some years by probably the best-known Latino political figure in the nation, Henry Cisneros. The city is almost one million in population and located at the fringe of central and south Texas. Although Houston is slightly further south, San Antonio is much closer to Mexico and the Texas–Mexico border.

For all of its charm and grace, San Antonio has been no more successful than other Texas cities in escaping ethnic and racial conflict. For much of the post–World War II period the city's politics were controlled by an establishment group known as the Good Government League (GGL). The GGL determined who would be elected to the city council. Although the GGL sometimes included Mexican Americans and blacks on its candidate slates, minorities never were represented in any number approaching their proportion of the population, nor were those minority candidates so designated likely to reflect socioeconomic backgrounds similar to that of the minority community at-large.

An attempt in the early 1970s to expand the at-large council and create a mixed electoral system was defeated by the voters in a referendum election. Then, following a series of annexations between 1972 and 1974, San Antonio was notified by the Justice Department that, due to the large Anglo populations in the annexed areas, the annexations would not be approved unless the city revised its electoral structure to include single-member districts.

Anxious to avoid a costly court suit, the city council placed another district plan on the local ballot. In January 1977, the new plan, creating a council of ten districts, was approved by a slim majority of the voters. The first elections were held in the spring of 1977 (for a complete history of this period in San Antonio politics, see Johnson et al. 1983). The first district council consisted of five Mexican Americans, five Anglos, and one black. The second council, after a very ugly and divisive period of fighting, resulted in an Anglo majority: four Mexican Americans, six Anglos, and one black. Astute observers of the San Antonio political scene suggest that the first postdistricted council simply went too far too fast in attempting to redistribute policy benefits to areas of the city that historically had been denied their fair share. The second council, and apparently subsequent councils, learned from this bitter lesson.

San Antonio was the first city without a large black population to sustain an annexation objection under the VRA. The GGL no longer slates or endorses candidates.

Following the 1990 census, the city redrew its council districts. The new council districts were drawn by a council committee with the assistance of city staff as well as other input. Apparently the process was not disruptive. One of the stated goals of the redistricting was to keep one safe black district. It apparently was felt that this was necessary to keep balance on the council. Although San Antonio today still has vestiges of ethnic conflict, most of the recent conflict has been between progressive-development forces and anti-tax-and-spend forces.

Victoria

Victoria is a relatively small (about 50,000) city with about one-third of its population Mexican American, located about two-thirds of the way from the Mexican border to Houston. It shares with New Braunfels an environment that includes Anglo, Mexican American, and German cultures. It is a relatively closed and frugal community, with a reputation for tight city budgets. During the 1970s eight minorities sought seats on the city council; none was elected.

In the spring of 1980 the city council appointed a charter revision committee to make recommendations concerning the city's electoral structure. At the time the city council was composed of a mayor and five councilpersons, all elected at-large. The ten-person revision committee included four minority members (three Mexican Americans).

The committee met through the summer of 1980, and heard comments from representatives of the NAACP, LULAC, and the Mexican American Chamber of Commerce, all of whom urged a change to single-member districts.

Although no suit had been filed, the committee was aware of the possibility of litigation. The chair of the committee, a former mayor, announced that "no recommendations would be made as a result of any threatened . . . litigation, [but rather recommendations] would be made simply on the basis of what was in the best interests of the city."

During the committee's deliberations, the two LULAC councils in Victoria took "informal" polls of the Mexican American neighborhoods and reported strong support for districts. The NAACP noted that with districts a councilperson "wouldn't have to go all the way across town to find out what the problems are."

In Fall 1980, the revision committee recommended a mixed system to avoid the worst aspects of "ward politics." One of the Mexican Americans on the committee filed a minority report, arguing for a council of all districts.

On January 17, 1981, the city voters ratified the charter revision, creating a council of six council seats, three at-large and three districted, plus a mayor elected at-large. The local newspaper had endorsed the change, noting that the purpose of the change was "to afford better representation for all sectors of our city" and "to enhance the opportunity for minority candidates to be elected to the city council."

The first elections were held in the spring of 1981. The first elections after the change produced some minority candidates and minority winners, although not at a proportional level. Most observers rate the hybrid council as producing little change. After the 1990 census, the Victoria city council redrew the districts, under some pressure from MALDEF. The plan was a compromise between one of pure districts and the hybrid of at-large and districts. The city was divided into four districts; these four districts were folded into two "super districts," creating a council of six, all from districts, but two from much larger districts. The first election under this plan was held in 1992.

Summary

Our focus of inquiry is on the impact of changing the electoral structures of city councils and school boards from at-large to district systems. We examine these changes in light of their impact on the Mexican American communities throughout Texas. In addition to aggregate data on Texas cities and schools, we employ a case study method and track ten Texas cities that have changed their election systems.

The impetus for much of this research comes from our interest in the impact of the Voting Rights Act on the Mexican American community. As already noted, the application of the VRA to Texas has been significant; more objections have been filed under the VRA with respect to Texas voting practices than those for any other state. The initial goal of the VRA was to facilitate minority voter registration. It has done that and much more. We turn now to an examination of both the history of the VRA and its current status.

Notes

1. For an overall assessment of the impact of the VRA, see the special issue of *Publius* (Fall 1986). A closer look at the "revisionist" criticisms of the VRA is found in chapter 2.

2. This is not because states such as North Carolina and Florida have not tried. See *Shaw* v. *Reno*, 1993.

2

The Jurisprudence of Voting

Right or wrong, we don't aim to let [blacks] vote. We just don't aim to let 'em vote.

quoted in V. O. Key,
Southern Politics in State and Nation

For Mexican Americans and blacks, voting has been historically an act of courage, not of citizenship. Well-documented measures, ranging from legal and economic sanctions to physical intimidation, have been employed over the decades to disenfranchise racial and ethnic minorities. The most direct attack on voting discrimination in the twentieth century came in 1965, when Congress passed the Voting Rights Act, and the attack has continued through the subsequent amendments to the VRA. Because the Voting Rights Act has been the impetus for much of the change we explore in this book, we turn now to an examination of the VRA and its impact on voting rights jurisprudence.

Pre–Voting Rights Act Jurisprudence

Voting is an inherent principle of democratic decision making. There is, however, no explicit recognition of this in the original constitution adopted in 1789. Justice William Douglas asserted in *Baker* v. *Carr*[1] that "the right to vote is inherent in the republican form of government envisaged by Article IV, Section 4 of the Constitution," but not until the adoption in 1870 of the Fifteenth Amendment did the right to vote find an explicit home in the U.S. Constitution.

In 1875, the U.S. Supreme Court recognized this right in *U.S.* v. *Reese,*[2] when it noted that "the [Fifteenth Amendment] has invested the citizens of the United States with a new constitutional right"

(*Reese*, 217). And, while *Reese* seemed to recognize that this right extended to blacks—which, after all, was the clear purpose of the amendment—the end of Reconstruction witnessed a series of decisions that rendered the Fifteenth Amendment impotent.[3]

Almost a century would pass between the ratification of the Fifteenth Amendment and the passage of the Voting Rights Act, a period that would demonstrate "the difficulty of implementing the policy of fair and effective voting for all citizens when a large segment of society opposes such a concept" (LeVarsky 1987, 303). The relatively few court decisions concerning voting rights during this time focused on the right to vote in a literal sense; that is, voting rights jurisprudence centered on the issue of vote denial. Beginning in the 1940s, the Supreme Court began to define the Fifteenth Amendment's scope of protection more aggressively. The foundation for the Court's position was laid in *Smith* v. *Allright*.[4] In striking down the whites-only primary system used in Texas elections, the Court noted that the right to vote was a "great privilege," and should not be denied to any person because of his or her race.

That legal position, however, ran head on into the political reality of the segregated South. The elimination of the white primaries simply shifted the focus of voting discrimination away from an outright denial of the vote at the door of the polling place to other measures designed to ensure that racial and ethnic minorities never attempted to go to the polling places. The measures included economic and physical intimidation. As a consequence, voter registration among blacks remained much lower than that of the white population, and voter turnout among blacks was almost nonexistent.

The Mexican American experience is somewhat different. There is not a wealth of data concerning Mexican American voter registration and turnout prior to 1975, but what there is indicates that Mexican Americans in general were more active than blacks (Grebler, Moore, and Guzman 1970; McCleskey and Merrill 1973; McCleskey and Nimmo 1968). As de la Garza and DeSipio note, in some cases Mexican American registration and turnout levels actually exceeded those of Anglos (1993, 1491). This latter finding may seem somewhat surprising, but in south Texas, for example, highly organized local political groups historically have been adept at turning out the ethnic vote.

In 1957 Congress passed the first civil rights bill since Reconstruction. This act represented the first modern attempt to protect the Fifteenth Amendment rights by creating a commission to investigate claims of vote denial (LeVarsky 1987, 306). The act was mostly of symbolic value, with little enforcement power, but it represented a break with the past and facilitated later action. In 1960 Congress expanded the power of the attorney general to protect black voters, and the 1964 Civil Rights Act included provisions expediting voting rights litigation. The Supreme Court also broke with the past during this period. The reapportionment decisions would establish a new view of the right to vote, one that would anticipate the dramatic shift from a jurisprudence focusing on vote denial to one focusing on vote dilution.

In 1962 the Court established fairness of representation as a justiciable issue with the landmark decision of *Baker* v. *Carr*. Although *Baker* was a procedural decision and did not speak to an explicit constitutional remedy for unfair representation, it established that, contrary to previous jurisprudence established by the Court, the right to vote in a context other than vote denial was a justiciable right. In essence, the prohibition of vote dilution is rooted in *Baker* v. *Carr* (McDonald 1989, 1258). The decision linked the Fourteenth Amendment protections to Fifteenth Amendment case law to support the discovery of "population-based voting rights" (Blacksher and Menefee 1982, 6–7).

Then, in 1964, the Court decided *Reynolds* v. *Sims*[5] and, in effect, and almost certainly without intent, laid the groundwork for much of the litigation that would spring from the adoption of the VRA a year later. In *Reynolds*, while discussing the application of the one-person, one-vote principle to state legislatures, the Court noted:

> There is more to the right to vote than the right to mark a piece of paper and drop it in a box or the right to pull a lever in a voting booth. The right to vote includes the right to have the ballot counted. . . . It also includes the right to have the vote counted at *full value without dilution or discount*. . . . [This] federally protected right suffers substantial dilution . . . [when a] favored group has full voting strength [and] the group not in favor have their votes discounted. (*Reynolds*, 555, n. 29, emphasis added)

Following the path of *Baker*, *Reynolds* merged the Fifteenth Amendment's prohibition against racial vote disenfranchisement with the Fourteenth Amendment's equal protection clause to find an "unspoken principle proscribing undervaluation of citizens' votes resulting from improper apportionment" (Blacksher and Menefee 1982, 3).

Reynolds expanded the notion of equal voting rights "to include any form of . . . diluting the strength of a citizen's vote" by "any method or means" (*Reynolds*, 563).

Shortly before the passage of the VRA, the Court recognized more explicitly that voting strength could be diluted on the basis of race as well as population equality in *Fortson* v. *Dorsey*.[6] Indeed, the Court observed that population equality among representative districts could be achieved, thus meeting the one-person, one-vote requirement, while, at the same time, racial minorities would have no chance of winning an election under the newly drawn districts (Blacksher and Menefee 1982, 18).

Prior to the passage of the VRA, these references to voter dilution attracted little attention in the courts. The jurisprudence concerning voting rights continued to focus on population equality and the application of the one-person, one-vote rule. When race was involved in a voting rights question, the courts continued to center on the issue of vote denial, rather than vote dilution. Although the Fifteenth Amendment was linked to the Fourteenth Amendment's equal protection clause to form the predicate for much of the reapportionment jurisprudence, the courts, with a curious and perhaps ironic touch, used it primarily to support the assertion of population-based voting rights, rather than racially based voting rights. This would change with the adoption of the VRA.

The Voting Rights Act

The Voting Rights Act of 1965[7] is considered the most important civil rights legislation in history (Ducat and Chase 1988, 744). Its impact on the political processes of various regions of the nation is impossible to exaggerate. The original act changed the political face of the Deep South, and subsequent amendments have resulted in dramatic changes in racial and ethnic political relationships throughout the Southwest and into California. Put simply, the VRA has translated the promise of the Fifteenth Amendment into political reality, albeit a reality far beyond that envisioned by the framers of the Civil War amendment.

The immediate impetus for the passage of the VRA came in March 1965, when the march on Selma, Alabama, resulted in nationally televised police violence against the marchers. A week later, President Lyndon Johnson, vowing that "we shall overcome," called on Congress to enact legislation protecting the rights of blacks to vote. With remarkable dispatch, Congress responded, and on August 6, 1965, President Johnson signed the VRA into law.

The act established two criteria that would trigger coverage: first, any jurisdictions that used a literacy test and, second, any jurisdictions with a voter turnout below 50 percent of the voting-age population in the 1964 presidential election were "covered jurisdictions." The VRA employed multiple weapons against covered jurisdictions, including the suspension of literacy tests, the provision of federal examiners to oversee voter registration, the imposition of criminal sanctions against those who intimidated people trying to vote, and the prohibition of poll taxes.

The most significant aspect of the act in the long run would turn out to be the Section 5 requirement that any change in the electoral systems of the covered jurisdictions be "precleared" with the Department of Justice. At the time of the act's passage the importance of the preclearance requirement was not recognized, but it would become the basis for much of the early litigation spawned by the VRA.

The clear target of the VRA was the South; the major provisions of the original act applied to six southern states in their entirety, most of a seventh southern state, and a few counties elsewhere. As McDonald (1989, 1251) observes, the initial focus of the act was "narrow, specialized, regional and racial." The implementation of the VRA centered on the voter registration process; the "sole concern" of those who wrote the statute was to remove the obstacles to registration and voting then placed in the paths of southern blacks (Thernstrom 1987, 4).

The South, however, had never lacked ingenuity when it came to disenfranchising the black population. In response to the VRA, the southern states erected more sophisticated forms of discrimination. Most important, southern jurisdictions shifted their focus away from voter registration to adopting measures that would ensure that, even though blacks might be able to register and vote, they could not win. These measures included malapportionment, gerrymandering, and the use of at-large election systems (LeVarsky 1987, 311). The judicial response to these tactics would dramatically expand the impact of the VRA.

Although the VRA was permanent legislation, some of its most important provisions were temporary, including the Section 5 preclearance provision that required preclearance with the Department of Justice of every new voting qualification or prerequisite to voting. The temporary provisions originally were intended to expire in five years.

This was a political tradeoff that recognized the dramatic departure from the traditional federal relationship between the national government and the states that the VRA represented. The powers embraced by the VRA had historically been exercised by the states; the sponsors of the bill recognized that they did not have the votes to pass the legislation if they gave these portions of the bill permanent status (Thernstrom 1987, 18). In effect, however, these provisions have been rendered permanent by the subsequent extensions of the act, and, indeed, the 1975 and 1982 amendments to the act have expanded its reach.

The first extension of the VRA occurred in 1970.[8] The focus of the act remained on blacks. Covered jurisdictions would be those that had utilized a literacy test and had less than 50 percent of the voting-age residents registered by the time of the 1968 presidential election. As a result of the new thresholds, the VRA extended to four counties with Latino populations (de la Garza and DeSipio 1993, 1481).

In 1975, the VRA and its jurisdictional coverage were extended for seven years. The temporary ban on the use of literacy tests was made permanent, and bailout provisions for covered jurisdictions were established. These latter provisions outlined the requirements by which covered jurisdictions, acting over a period of time in good faith to remedy past sins, could achieve a state of grace sufficient to exclude them from continued monitoring by the feds. The 1975 VRA also allowed individuals, as well as the Justice Department, to bring suit under the act.

Most significantly, the 1975 amendments extended the coverage of the act to four "language minorities": those of Spanish heritage, Native Americans, Asian Americans, and Alaskan natives. In addition to the application of the preclearance and federal observer protections to language minorities, the 1975 VRA required that bilingual election materials be provided in jurisdictions where more than 5 percent of a single language minority and an illiteracy rate of the language minority higher than the national average existed.

As de la Garza and DeSipo note, (1993, 1483) the testimony offered by Mexican American witnesses in support of the extension of the act were qualitative generalizations concerning voter discrimination against Mexican Americans supported by minimal quantitative evidence. Quantitative support was unnecessary, as Congress accepted the testimony establishing a pattern of systematic discrimination against Mexican Americans, particularly in Texas, even though there was some question as to whether Mexican Americans actually were being disenfranchised (Thernstrom 1987, 57).

In bringing specific language minorities under the umbrella of the VRA, Congress altered the act in a way that would significantly affect the voting rights jurisprudence. First, since the Fifteenth Amendment protections were predicated on race and not language identities, the base of the VRA was expanded to include the Fourteenth Amendment. Second, the primary focus of the 1975 protections to language minorities was not centered on overt voter disenfranchisement, but rather on voter dilution, "on electoral arrangements that gave minority voters 'unequal' electoral power" (Thernstrom 1987, 58).

The VRA was extended again in 1982.[9] Congress, reacting to the Supreme Court's ruling in *City of Mobile* v. *Bolden,*[10] establishing that an intent to discriminate was necessary to activate VRA coverage, amended Section 2 of the VRA so that a "results" test rather than an "intents" test was required to trigger the bill's protection. The requirement that bilingual election materials be provided was extended for ten years, and the preclearance provisions for twenty-five years.

The Section 2 amendments would have far-reaching consequences for voting rights jurisprudence. Section 2 and Section 5's preclearance requirements would become the twin foundations for most voting rights litigation following 1982.

The final extension of the VRA to date occurred in 1992. The bilingual provisions were renewed for fifteen years, and the requirements that bilingual election materials be provided were expanded to include localities with populations of at least 10,000 of any of the covered language minorities. The result was that several major cities (e.g., Los Angeles, San Francisco) were added to the covered jurisdictions.

Thus, in the years since the VRA's initial passage, Congress has amended and extended the act four times. Each time, Congress has expanded and increased the protection provided by the act. Not surprisingly, these expansions have affected the judicial perception of the act's coverage. We turn now to an examination of voting rights jurisprudence following the adoption of the VRA.

VRA Jurisprudence: The First Stage

The legislative focus of the VRA seemed clear. The act was designed to attack practices in the southern states that obstructed African

Americans' access to the ballot. The primary attacks were directed at the southern opposition to black voter registration, particularly at the use of literacy tests. The debates surrounding the adoption of the Section 5 preclearance provisions clearly envision preclearance as a means of ensuring the removal of literacy tests or other devices that might keep blacks from voting (Thernstrom 1987, 20–30).

The early jurisprudence concerning the application of the VRA, however, quickly moved the Section 5 preclearance provision to the front burner, and, in so doing, shifted the focus of the act from voter access to vote dilution. This process began with *Allen* v. *State Board of Elections,*[11] a consolidation of four cases, one of which involved Mississippi legislation allowing counties to replace district elections with at-large structures. Since such changes did not inhibit access to voting by black voters, there was a question as to whether the VRA's preclearance requirements were applicable. Chief Justice Earl Warren quickly disposed of the issue and changed the course of voting rights jurisprudence. The Chief Justice noted:

> The Voting Rights Act was aimed at the subtle, as well as the obvious, state regulations which would have the effect of denying citizens their right to vote because of race. . . . [T]he right to vote can be affected by a dilution of voting power as well as by an absolute prohibition on casting a ballot. (*Allen,* 565, 569)

In dissent, Justice John Marshall Harlan, Jr., referred to the legislative history of the VRA to contend that if Section 5 were to be interpreted as the majority opinion intended, this would allow federal authorities to prohibit the introduction of new methods of electoral structures, rather than prohibit only those procedures that kept blacks from the polls (*Allen,* 584). Harlan was correct in both his reading of the legislative intent and the consequences of the decision.

As Thernstrom notes, the *Allen* decision separates the preclearance requirements from their intended relationship to the literacy tests. The Court had made a "radical" change in the meaning of the VRA: "the majority opinion had found a Fourteenth Amendment right to protection from vote dilution in a statute that rested unequivocally on the Fifteenth Amendment" (Thernstrom 1987, 24–25).

Still, Warren's opinion was hardly developed from whole cloth. Both the *Baker* and the *Reynolds* decisions recognized Fourteenth and

Fifteenth Amendment links as well as the relationship of vote dilution to the right to vote. The Mississippi statute clearly was intended to remove the ability of blacks to use their votes to win elections; a voting rights act in name only could be construed to permit such action.

The Court's decision in *Allen* paved the way for the VRA to become the most significant civil rights act in history. This was the first broad interpretation of the preclearance requirements and shifted the protection of the act to vote dilution as well as vote denial (Engstrom 1978, 144). Without this construction of the Section 5 preclearance provisions, the VRA's impact on black voting rights would be much narrower, and it is unlikely it would have had much impact at all on other minorities.

By the 1970s, VRA litigation focused more on vote dilution than on vote denial. The dilution of minority voting strength was not tested directly on the merits until 1971 in *Whitcomb v. Chavis*.[12] At issue was Indiana's legislative apportionment and a question as to whether multimember districts diluted black voting strength. Although the Court upheld the reapportionment, it acknowledged that minority voting rights were protected from vote dilution created by multimember districts, but it did not indicate the basis for proof of vote dilution (Kosterlitz 1987, 537).

This acknowledgment was translated into action in *White v. Regester*.[13] Here black and Mexican American plaintiffs challenged a portion of Texas's 1970 reapportionment plan for the Texas House of Representatives. The Court, relying heavily on a historical context that spoke to decades of voting discrimination against blacks and cultural discrimination against Mexican Americans, struck down the use of multimember districts as impermissibly diluting the right to vote.

At the same time, the majority opinion lacked "coherence" (Thernstrom 1987, 71). Consequently, the Court did not develop a cohesive rationale that the lower courts could apply against minority vote dilution (Blacksher and Menefee 1982, 19). The Court did identify several factors that might be used by lower courts in determining whether vote dilution existed. These included history, majority vote requirements, lack of minority electoral success, candidate slating, and racial appeals during campaigns. The Court also talked of a standard using the "totality of circumstances" to substantiate a claim of dilution (*White*, 769).

The quest for guidelines concerning vote dilution seemingly ended with *Zimmer v. McKeithen*,[14] decided three months after *White*. *Zim-*

mer involved an attempt by a Louisiana parish to replace its district election structure for parishwide and school board seats with an at-large scheme. Black voters objected and their claims were sustained by the Fifth Circuit. *Zimmer* categorized the factors mentioned in *White* as guidelines for future court decisions concerning vote dilution. *Zimmer* recognized two elements necessary to a concept of fair representation. First, the one-person, one-vote rule must obtain. Second, "assuming substantial equality, the [election scheme] must not operate to minimize or cancel out the voting strength of racial elements of the voting population" (*Zimmer*, 1303). The latter would be determined by examining two sets of factors: primary and enhancing. Primary factors included lack of access by minorities to the process of slating candidates, unresponsiveness of legislators to the particularized interests of minority voters, a tenuous state policy underlying their preference for multi-member or at-large districting, and the existence of past discrimination that precluded effective minority participation. The importance of any of the primary factors was considered "enhanced" when any combination of the following factors existed: large districts, majority vote requirements, anti-single-shot voting provisions, and an absence of geographical subdistricts.

Zimmer, extending *White*, provided the judiciary with an explicit guide to use to determine the existence of vote dilution. And, although the precise weights given to the *Zimmer* "checklist" might vary from court to court, it is fair to say that the *Zimmer* criteria were the basis for determining voter dilution from 1973 to 1980.

The Supreme Court, while reserving judgment on *Zimmer*'s theory of vote dilution, did recognize the *Zimmer* factors in *East Carroll Parish School Bd.* v. *Marshall*[15] in 1976. Still, it became increasingly clear during the mid- to late 1970s that the Court was reexamining the reach of Section 5.[16] Most important, the Court was addressing the critical issue of intent versus effect or result. That is, jurisdictions began to contend that their election systems should be judged infirm only if it could be shown that they had been adopted for the express purpose of diluting the minority vote. The fact that an election scheme might result in vote dilution would not be sufficient to impeach its legitimacy absent a finding of intent, the aggregate factors in *Zimmer* notwithstanding. The adoption of such a test would place a heavier burden on plaintiffs to establish vote dilution.

In 1980, the Court decided *Mobile* v. *Bolden*[17] and ended the first stage of VRA jurisprudence. Mobile, Alabama, used an at-large election scheme to elect its city commissioners. Although one-third of the city's population was black, no black had ever been elected to the commission. Black plaintiffs challenged the at-large scheme and won at both the district court and the Fifth Circuit. The Supreme Court reversed, however, and instituted an intents test. The Court required the plaintiffs to demonstrate that the adoption of the at-large system was intended to keep them from winning elections. The Court also rejected the use of the aggregate factors outlined by *Zimmer* (Kosterlitz 1987, 540). Finally, the Court also turned away from the "totality-of-circumstances" test employed in *White* (*Mobile*, 63).

The *Mobile* decision focused on the VRA rather than on the Fourteenth Amendment. The Court contended that Section 2 of the VRA served to codify the Fifteenth Amendment and, as such, that Section 2 required plaintiffs to meet the Fifteenth Amendment's standard of purposeful discrimination (*Mobile*, 63).

While *Mobile* rejected the *White* and *Zimmer* jurisprudence, it was unable to establish clear guidelines as to how the lower courts were to determine invidious intent to discriminate. Justice White, who continued to urge adherence to the totality-of-circumstances test (which he had authored in *White*), observed that *Mobile* did not provide a clear substitute for the *Zimmer* guidelines; Justice White asserted that *Mobile* "leaves the courts below adrift on uncharted seas with respect to how to proceed" (*Mobile*, 103).

There was nationwide criticism of *Mobile* (McDonald 1989, 1267), and two years later Congress amended Section 2 of the VRA to require a results test. Voting rights jurisprudence would shift now from Section 5 preclearance activity to Section 2 litigation.

VRA Jurisprudence: The Second Stage

The revision of Section 2 to reinstate a results rather than an intents test placed plaintiffs back in the driver's seat. The clear result of Congress was to "lighten the plaintiff's burden of proof" (Miller and Packman 1987, 3).

Following the 1982 amendments, the lower courts continually found for the plaintiffs; at-large election schemes began to become endangered species. The jurisprudence, however, was not as cohesive as the rulings; guidelines varied between the circuits and between courts within circuits (Kosterlitz 1987, 544). The Fifth and Eleventh circuits tended to use a "hierarchical approach" emphasizing polarized voting, while the Fourth Circuit returned to *White*'s totality-of-circumstances standard, adopting a more "stringent" definition of polarized voting (Kosterlitz 1987, 548).

The Supreme Court attempted to resolve some of these differences in 1986 with its decision in *Thornburg* v. *Gingles*.[18] Here, the Court, speaking through Justice William Brennan, established a three-part test for applying Section 2 challenges to election systems. The at-large schemes would be illegal if (1) the minority population were sufficiently segregated residentially to afford the remedy of single-member districts with a majority minority population, (2) the minority group must be politically cohesive, and (3) the white majority must vote sufficiently as a bloc to enable it to defeat the minority's preferred candidates. The remedy for such a scheme was the requirement of district elections. A plurality of the Court also focused on the race or ethnicity of the voter as a determining factor, rather than the race or ethnicity of the candidates.

The key to vote dilution claims was the existence of racial or ethnic bloc voting. The Court recognized four general principles to determine the degree of racial polarization: (1) a showing that a minority group is cohesive and generally votes for the same candidate; (2) the presence of white or Anglo bloc voting sufficient to defeat minority candidates; (3) a historical pattern of bloc voting; and (4) an exception to the historical pattern that does not sustain an attack on the bloc voting argument (Kosterlitz 1987, 555). The emphasis on polarized voting was unexpected; it had not been mentioned in *White* or *Zimmer*, nor had it received much attention during the legislative debates over the 1982 amendments to Section 2 (Jacobs and O'Rourke 1986, 301–8).

Thornburg clearly moved the 1986 application of the VRA some distance from that envisioned in 1965. LeVarsky (1987, 322) suggests that the opinion leads to a reasonable conclusion that voters should have an equal opportunity to influence an election result. The debates a generation ago over access to the polls seem almost arcane now as virtually all voting rights litigation focuses on vote dilution rather than vote denial.

Thornburg, although it set the tone for voting rights jurisprudence through the 1992 VRA amendments, did not establish crystal-clear standards for the lower courts to follow. This may, of course, be both a strength and a weakness: a weakness in the sense that it is generally considered desirable that there be uniform guidelines directing judicial decisions across the nation; a strength in that it is unlikely, even if it were desirable, that an issue as complex as voting rights can be fit into a single straitjacket of judicial guidelines. *Thornburg* recognized as much when the Court acknowledged that there is no "simple doctrinal test for the existence of legally significant racial bloc voting" (*Thornburg*, 55–56).

Sushma Soni (1990, 1652) has observed that, while *Thornburg* was designed to "pull order out of litigation chaos . . . and to rein in the discretion afforded by section 2, while remaining consistent with the legislative intent behind the amendments, . . . the Justices failed to agree on several crucial definitions." And LeVarsky (1987, 328) acknowledges that the greatest difficulty with *Thornburg* lies in the Court's failure to concretely describe when each of the elements of racially polarized voting is met.

Nonetheless, *Thornburg* does seem to have given greater judicial control over the direction of minority vote litigation by focusing on polarized voting. In addition, the case removed any "lingering doubts" about the use of single-member districts as a remedy for infirm at-large systems by requiring this as *the* remedy (McDonald 1989, 1273).

Perhaps most obviously, *Thornburg* accelerated the pace at which the VRA was being applied to covered jurisdictions. The combination of the 1982 amendments to Section 2 with *Thornburg* has served to intensify the application of the VRA to local governments throughout the South and Southwest. Plaintiffs do not win all of the time, but their rate of success is sufficiently high that jurisdictions often avoid litigation (and litigation costs) by agreeing prior to the filing of a law suit to replace their at-large election systems with districted or mixed schemes. As we move to the end of this century, *Thornburg* continues to inform the voting rights jurisprudence. At the same time, a revisionist interpretation of *Thornburg* and the VRA has emerged that gives promise of charging the debate for the next few years.

Future VRA Jurisprudence: The Revisionist Position

In general, the revisionist interpretation of *Thornburg* contends that the decision casts too narrow a shadow. Abrams (1988, 472) calls for a jurisprudence of "political opportunity" that recognizes that Congress's intent in amending Section 2 was to go beyond just the right to electoral success. There is support for this interpretation in the language of the amended Section 2, which refers to the openness of the "political processes leading to nomination or election" and the equal opportunity to participate in those processes, as well as the opportunity "to elect representatives of [the minority voters'] own choice."[19]

The argument is that preelection and postelection political activities are as important as the issue of vote dilution. Section 2, the revisionists contend, is concerned not just with broadening political participation through the electoral process, but also with addressing "the patterns and effects of societal discrimination" (Abrams 1988, 475). The emphasis of *Thornburg* on electoral success thus "prevents the courts from fully achieving the goals of the 1982 amendments to the Voting Rights Act" (Carstarphen 1991, 405). That is, minorities can accomplish political objectives through activities other than voting, such as political discussion, lobbying, and coalition building. Each of the latter activities is protected by Section 2 through its guarantee of an equal opportunity to participate in the political process (Carstarphen 1991, 413).

Thornburg's reliance on the remedy of single-member districts runs counter to both the language of Section 2 and the intent of Congress. The Section 2 amendments were intended to accomplish three goals: (1) to replace the intents test with a results test, (2) to elect officials who are more responsive to minorities, and (3) to incorporate minority voters into the political process. The latter goal especially goes beyond the electoral arena; equal opportunity at the ballot is not the equivalent of equal opportunity to participate in the political process (Shockley 1991, 1053–60).

From a practical standpoint, the revisionists argue, the focus on single-member districts in effect encourages residential segregation and makes it difficult for residentially dispersed minorities to seek protection from Section 2. This, they point out, ignores the "critical connection between broad-based sustained voter participation and accountable representation" (Guinier 1991, 1080). Thus, *Thornburg* may produce a more representative government, but not necessarily a more responsive government. That is, city councils and school boards may end up with minority members where none sat before, but the numerical disadvantage at which these minority members find themselves (e.g., as one member of a five-member city council), combined with a community where ethnicity or race is not residentially cohesive, reduces their effectiveness at translating their elections into effective policy outcomes for the minority community.

In somewhat the same vein, de la Garza and DeSipio (1993, 1514–1516) note that the drawing of single-member districts with majority Mexican American populations, while increasing Mexican American representation, has come at a cost to Mexican American political participation. That is, there has not been an increase in Mexican American voter turnout, since the emphasis of the VRA has been on who gets elected rather than on who votes. Therefore, if the VRA was intended to strengthen the "linkage between the electorate and the electoral system" through "increased minority electoral participation," it has failed to do so with reference to Latino voters.

Thus, the revisionists' call for a change in voting rights jurisprudence centers on two general criticisms of *Thornburg*. First, the current reliance on single-member districts is too narrow a remedy and ignores both statutory language and congressional intent. Second, the use of single-member districts may not result in a more responsive government in that minority voters may be cut off from the broader political community and minority voter turnout may actually decrease following the change to district elections. Single-member districts emphasize what Abrams (1988, 488) calls the "preference aggregation" model instead of what she considers the more desirable, and more broadly based, "interactive participation" model. Continuing down a similar path, Shockley (1991, 1059) calls for a jurisprudence focusing more on "civic inclusion" and "civic participation," a call supported by Guinier (1991), Abrams (1988), and Karlan (1989).

It is not easy to assess the impact of the revisionist arguments. Academic arguments endure considerable lag times between their initial appearances and their acceptance in the public arena. At the same time, voting rights litigation almost always employs the testimony of expert witnesses, most of whom come from the academy. As a result, discussions of alternatives to districting as the sole remedy for voting rights dilution are likely to increase, and such remedies as cumulative voting, restrictive voting, and the single transferable vote are receiving attention.

It seems likely, and desirable, therefore, that this recent scholarship addressing current voting rights jurisprudence will encourage the courts to continue to refine the meaning of the VRA. Already, some lower courts are attempting to resolve the potential conflict between

Thornburg's reliance on single-member districts and vote dilution claims brought by residentially dispersed minorities.[20]

We suspect there may be growing support for a broadening of the available remedies to racial and ethnic vote dilution. The remedy should fit the situation, and if the situation dictates a remedy other than single-member districting, then so be it. However, the idea that single-member districting encourages residential segregation puts the cart before the horse. Residential segregation throughout the Southwest is not a result of single-member districting, but rather of systemic discrimination against racial and ethnic minorities over much of the region's history.

Similarly, we are less persuaded by de la Garza's and DiSipio's complaint that increased representation coming at a cost of decreased participation is an undesirable tradeoff. Decreased participation may be a function of incumbency and a lack of competition. This incumbency, however, likely is a function of the change from at-large elections, in which Mexican American incumbents were as rare as a humble Texan, to districts where Mexican American incumbents, if not a common sight, are no longer a conversation item. We believe that most Mexican American voters would choose this tradeoff at the drop of a hat.

As these academics have been exploring the nuances of the VRA, the U.S. Supreme Court has been engaging in a bit of revisionism on its own. On June 28, 1993, the Court decided *Shaw* v. *Reno*.[21] North Carolina, acting under direction from the U.S. Department of Justice and seeking to comply with Section 5 of the VRA, had drawn a congressional district so as to guarantee a district with a significant African American population advantage. In order to accomplish that goal, however, the district had to be drawn in a highly irregular shape, so irregular that for much of the district's length it was no wider than an interstate highway. Indeed, as was widely quoted, one North Carolina legislator observed that "[i]f you drove down the interstate with both car doors open, you'd kill most of the people in that district."[22] Northbound and southbound drivers on I–85 found themselves in separate districts in one county, only to change districts upon entering an adjacent county.

Speaking for the Court in the 5–4 decision, Justice Sandra Day O'Connor noted that the case addressed two of the most "complex and sensitive" issues the Court had faced in recent years: "the meaning of the constitutional right to vote, and the propriety of race-based state legislation designed to benefit members of historically disadvantaged racial minority groups" (*Shaw*, 2819). The Court then sent the case back to a lower federal court to determine whether the sole justification for the peculiar lines of the district rested on race, and, if so, whether the racial gerrymander could be justified as furthering a compelling governmental interest. O'Connor noted that "[c]lassifications of citizens solely on the basis of race are by their very nature odious to a free people" (*Shaw*, 2824). She said further, "[a] reapportionment plan that includes in one district individuals who belong to the same race, but who are otherwise widely separated by geographical and political boundaries, and who may have little in common with one another but the color of their skin, bears an uncomfortable resemblance to political apartheid" (*Shaw*, 2827). The Court noted that a covered jurisdiction's obligation to satisfy Section 5 requirements does not provide *carte blanche* to engage in racial gerrymandering.

The dissenters weren't buying any of this. Arguing, in general, that the majority opinion deviated from long-established precedent and, perhaps more important, that the "conscious use of race in redistricting does not violate the Equal Protection Clause unless the effect of the redistricting plan is to deny a particular group equal access to the political process or to minimize its voting strength unduly" (Blackmun at 2843), the minority contended that the lower court's decision to dismiss the original suit was justified.

The significance of *Shaw* probably is found more in its deviation from the long line of cases in which the Court has found little or no fault with racially gerrymandered districts drawn in response to voting rights litigation. The substantive significance of the case will have to await the disposal of the case by the lower court. It is true that the case seems to signal a departure from voting rights precedents, and perhaps portends a shift in the Court's willingness to continue to pursue racial gerrymandering as the sole remedy to VRA violations. At the same time, the North Carolina district was so egregiously erratic that it is highly unlikely that *Shaw* will prove a harbinger of dramatic change.

What is clear is that as the VRA moves into its second generation, the combination of the revisionists' positions and the uncertainty created by *Shaw* gives promise of a continually evolving jurisprudence.

That, however, speaks to the future. For our purposes this examination of the VRA has served as background for our analysis of the impact of the VRA on the Mexican American population in Texas.

Notes

1. 369 U.S. 186, at 242.
2. 92 U.S. 214.
3. For an examination of this period, see Derfner (1973).
4. 321 U.S. 649 (1944).
5. 377 U.S. 533.
6. 379 U.S. 433 (1965).
7. For a fuller treatment of the development of the VRA, see Harrell (1974) and Thernstrom (1987).
8. PL 91–285.
9. PL 97–205.
10. 446 U.S. 55
11. 393 U.S. 544 (1969).
12. 403 U.S. 124 (1971).
13. 412 U.S. 755 (1973).
14. 486 F. 2d 1297 (5th. Cir. 1973).
15. 434 U.S. 636 (1976).
16. See, particularly, *Lockhart* v. *U.S.*
17. 446 U.S. 55 (1980).
18. 476 U.S. 30 (1986).
19. 42 U.S. C. 8 1973b (1982).
20. See, for example, the conflict *East Jefferson Coalition* v. *Parish of Jefferson* (691 F. Supp. 991-E D. La., 1981), wherein the court extended Section 2 protection to dispersed minority voters, and *McNeil* v. *Springfield Park District* (851 F. 2d. 937, 7th Cir. 1988), wherein the court denied such protection. The U.S. Supreme Court denied certiorari in 1991.
21. 113 U.S. 2816 (1993).
22. *Washington Post*, April 20, 1993, A4.

3

Electoral Structure and Minority Representation: A General Description

The Rise of Mexican American Political Activity

The quest for Mexican American empowerment in Texas did not begin with the passage of the Voting Rights Act. The history of Texas is, in part, a history of a continuing struggle between the Mexican origin population and the Anglo population. The genesis of that struggle was the clash of cultures. Large numbers of Anglo Americans legally and illegally emigrated to Texas from the United States in the early nineteenth century, and the Spanish/Mexican majority in the Texas of the late eighteenth century quickly became a minority in their own land.

By 1834, thirty thousand Anglo Americans had arrived in Texas. *Tejanos* (Mexicans born in Texas) numbered only five thousand (McWilliams 1968, 89). According to De Leon (1993, 28), Tejanos originally welcomed the Anglo settlers. That attitude, however, soon changed. Most Anglo immigrants had come from the South and resented the Mexican government, which opposed slavery. They also resented the government's imposition of customs duties and its requirement that legal immigrants convert to Catholicism. McLemore and Romo (1985, 7–8) note, "The Anglos . . . increasingly failed to distinguish the *Tejanos* from the Mexican nationals with whom they were struggling, and, in the process, the ethnic boundary between the two groups was sharply drawn." Differences in language, religion, economic interests, levels of nationalism, and vision of the future exacerbated the hostility between the two groups. "To the early American settlers, the Mexicans were lazy, shiftless, jealous, cowardly, bigoted, superstitious, backward, and immoral" (McWilliams 1968, 99). Mexicans regarded Anglos as "arrogant, overbearing, aggressive, conniving, rude, unreliable, and dishonest" (McWilliams 1968, 99).

This pattern continued following the Texas Revolution in 1836. Mirande notes, "Anglo contempt of the Mexican during the Mexican period grew into open hatred and hostility following Texas independence" (1985, 24). Anglo perceptions of Mexican Americans as inferior became the dominant racial attitude.

The United States' annexation of Texas and the subsequent war between the United States and Mexico continued to fuel the flames of Anglo–Mexican distrust. The United States military occupation of a major portion of Mexico and the acquisition by the United States of California, Arizona, New Mexico, Texas, and portions of Colorado in 1846 by the Treaty of Guadalupe Hidalgo further reinforced the conflict. Numerous authors characterize the political history of this period as violent and suppressive (Acuna 1981; Anders 1982; Dickens 1969; Garcia and de la Garza 1977; McLemore and Romo 1985; McWilliams 1968; Mirande 1985; Montejano 1987). According to De Leon:

> In the 1850s, flagrant attacks upon Tejanos persisted as xenophobia, politics, and economic rivalries mixed and incited racial antipathy . . . [C]lashes between the races spread to the territory below the Nueces River as Anglos penetrated the South Texas frontier for the first time. Anglo arrogance and Texas–Mexican right became causes for contention. . . . Following the Civil War, lynchings and other barbarities perpetrated against Tejanos found renewed expression. South Texas became a powder keg of violence in the competition between profiteers from both sides of the border who sought to rustle cattle and mavericks from local ranches and the open South Texas range. (1993, 37–39)

Much of the violence stemmed from conflict over property. Throughout Texas, landowning Mexicans who remained in the United States, who under the Treaty of Guadalupe Hidalgo became U.S. citizens, and whose property rights were guaranteed by that treaty, were reduced from landowners to common laborers. Mirande (1985, 21) notes that, as happened elsewhere in the Southwest, a "massive change in landownership had been effected. As a result of force, armed conflict, legislative manipulation, and outright purchase, much of the land was now in Yankee hands." According to Acuna (1981, 30), "The new political order promoted capital accumulation. . . . Richard King . . . the arch-robber baron of South Texas . . . amassed over 600,000 acres of land during his lifetime, and his widow increased the family holdings to over 1,000,000 acres."

Tejanos found their claims to property under attack by an increasing number of Anglo settlers. Some were forced to flee to Mexico, and their lands were confiscated by Anglos (De Leon 1993, 37). Unable to redress their claims through the political system, Mexican Americans turned to other means. Interethnic violence and bloodshed were common during the latter half of the nineteenth century and early part of the twentieth century, especially along the Texas–Mexico border and in south Texas (Montejano 1987; McLemore and Romo 1985). Rosenbaum says that, "During the course of the nineteenth century, Mexicanos employed violence as one means of retaining some measure of self determination in the face of an increasingly oppressive new regime" (1981, 16). In Brownsville, Texas, Juan Cortina, a disenchanted landowner, initiated an open rebellion against the new political establishment in 1859. Operating ranches on both sides of the new border, Cortina and his followers launched raids for several years from Mexico into the United States. These raids, and others, by Mexican "border bandits" led to much violence and Anglo reprisals. Anders notes,

> The bands of desperados showed little disposition to differentiate along racial lines in choosing their victims. Unfortunately, Companies of Anglo militiamen perceived the upheaval as a racial conflict and turned their rage against countless innocent Mexican American victims. (1982, xv)

In 1915, Texas and the U.S. government, citing disturbances along the border, launched a major attack against Mexican Americans in the lower Rio Grande valley of south Texas. The Texas Rangers were prominent in these attacks, gaining a reputation for violence that would last among the Mexican American community throughout the twentieth century (Samora et al. 1979).

The "Americanization" of south Texas forced Tejanos into a subservient position; as in most other Southwestern states, Anglos dominated the political and economic institutions throughout the first half of the twentieth century. Mirande (1985, 23) observes that nowhere in the Southwest was the repression more intense than in Texas.

This Americanization process occurred in spite of the legal position of Mexican Americans. Clearly, as a result of the Treaty of Guadalupe Hidalgo, Mexican Americans were American citizens and had the right to vote. In fact, during the nineteenth century and early part of the twentieth century, the Mexican American community formed the base of political power in south Texas, often under the watchful eye of a *patrón* (Anders 1982). The *patrón* system, however, had lasting consequences for Anglo–Mexican American political relationships. Anders argues that the *patrón–peón* relationship that existed between large landowners and laborers helped structure attitudes toward political participation on the part of Mexican Americans (Anders 1982, xii): "Even with the elimination of the legal sanction for peonage after the collapse of Mexican rule, the tradition of paternalistic responsibility and willing subservience continued."

Dickens describes how the *patrón* system worked in San Antonio:

> [P]olitical bosses needed only to control the employer who, in turn, would tell "his Mexicans" how to vote. Under the patron system it was customary for Mexican Americans working for someone else to go to their employer and ask how to vote. Mexican Americans were not necessarily forced to vote a particular way, but they asked who to vote for as a sign of their loyalty, respect, and degree of faith in the employer or patron. (1969, 32)

Montejano (1987, 82) argues that the scarcity of work and need for protection from chronic lawlessness of the region also promoted the *patrón–peón* relationship. Acuna discusses how that system worked along the border region in south Texas:

> In South Texas, machine politics also became popular after the Civil War. The machine handed out patronage—for example, city jobs, contracts, franchises, and public utilities and, in the case of poor Mexicans, gave them a primitive form of welfare. The machine won elections by turning out the Mexican vote. In the border towns, the machine also controlled the custom houses. The indiscriminate use of the Texas Rangers bolstered the machine's political hegemony. (1981, 34)

The *peonage* tradition helped shape the rise of political leaders as "bosses" who maintained power with the support of the Mexican American community. Commenting on border politics in south Texas, Anders notes:

> Rather than offering an open society with abundant opportunity for improved living conditions and upward mobility, the Wells machine won Mexican American support by embracing the survivors of the Mexican elite and sustaining a social system to which most of the populace was accustomed. That system was certainly exploitative with the relegation of most Mexican Americans to low paying manual labor. Still the continuation of a familiar culture, the low level of overt racial discrimination, and the availability of paternalistic aid offered some compensations. . . . To mobilize their Hispanic support fully, the Cameron County Democrats took advantage of lax election laws and engaged in practices of questionable legality. (1982, 16)

The "practices of questionable legality" included holding large barbecues *(pachangas)*, where supporters would be given food and drink and then driven to the polls to vote for designated candidates (Anders 1982; Montejano 1987). At times this process included payments in the form of money. That these practices were common in the United States of the 1880s–1920s is fairly well known. And, the Mexican American vote was still accepted as legitimate. In the early part of the century, however, Anglo immigration into south Texas began to change the political landscape. With the settlement of the Rio Grande valley in the 1920s, Anglo "reformers" of south Texas began to establish even firmer control over the political processes. Montejano (1987, 130–31) says, "The condemnation of the Texas Mexican voter did not come simply because the [Anglo] newcomers found their attempts to develop the country frustrated. . . . They insisted on a new morality, a new code of social relations." The new morality of the Anglo immigrants included a new place for the Mexican American—one well below that of Anglos on the social scale and fairly impotent politically (Montejano 1987, 131). The Anglo takeover of south Texas resulted in a reorganization of the local governments—mainly an expansion of counties—and the virtual disenfranchisement of Mexican Americans (Montejano 1987, 133).

The disenfranchisement of Mexican Americans occurred over the course of several years in the early twentieth century. Among the major events were the establishment of the White Man's Primary Association (1914), the Texas legislative investigation of the 1919 Glasscock–Parr race, and the 1928 investigation of political activities in Hidalgo County (Montejano 1987, 143–48). These activities, as well as the establishment of the poll tax (1902), the direct primary (1903), and monolingual (English) ballots, helped to keep Mexican Americans away from the polls (Montejano 1987, 143). De Leon (1993, 30) notes that the Progressive movement institutionalized citywide elections and weakened bossism, "but in the process it eliminated the old ward system under which minorities had commanded at least some sort of representation." The impact of these devices and activities was not subtle. For example, the Mexican American population of Cameron County along the Texas–Mexico border exceeded 50 percent at the turn of the century. The number of Mexican Americans holding office in Cameron County dropped from slightly more than 50 percent in 1902 to less than 10 percent in 1922 (Binder and Garcia 1989).

Mobilization theory suggests that the subordinate group in such a situation would attempt to mobilize individuals and groups to respond collectively by applying their resources toward the acquisition of social and political goods (Morrison 1987). It is the level and type of resources available to minorities and other out-groups that allow the development of strategies and tactics to achieve goals (see Button 1989, 14). In fact, this is what happened. Shortly after control passed from the old regime based on Tejano community support, efforts were made to mobilize the Mexican Americans and to regain some facet of political power.

Mexican Americans had a common culture, language, and social tradition that could serve to mobilize the community (San Miguel 1987, 7). They also had a general agreement on values, especially the importance of education. Mobilization began to occur with the establishment of Mexican American organizations. Such groups as *Orden Hijos de America* (Sons of America Order) and *Orden Caballeros de America* (Knights of America Order) were established in San Antonio in the 1920s and were dedicated to nonviolent means of participation in society by Mexican Americans. Another group formed during this period was the League of United Latin American Citizens (LULAC), organized from several Mexican American groups in 1929 (San Miguel 1987, 68).[1] Garcia and de la Garza (1977, 27) identify the tenuous nature of the organization by its title. Instead of *Mexican,* the word *Latin* was used, and *Citizens* was added to emphasize the Americanness of the organization. LULAC was a conservative, accommodationist organization aimed at promoting the interests of the Mexican American middle class (Garcia and de la Garza 1977, 28). The promotion of educational standards for Mexican Americans was a primary goal of the organization.

Prior to World War II, LULAC was the most prominent Latino political organization. Following the war, numerous organizations developed in response to the need to pursue Mexican American empowerment. These included the G.I. Forum, Viva Kennedy, PASO, and MAYO. In the 1970s, *La Raza Unida*, a political party, successfully contested selected municipal elections and offered statewide candidates in two gubernatorial elections. While all of these organizations aided in the political mobilization of the Mexican American community, the emergence of the Mexican American Legal Defense and Education Fund (MALDEF) and the Southwest Voter Registration and Education Project (now Southwest Voter) would play the most critical role in using the VRA (expanded to cover language minorities in 1975) to assert Mexican American political claims in the cities of the Southwest. Beginning in the 1970s, these organizations would argue before the courts that the at-large election systems diluted Mexican American voting strength and that the proper remedy under the VRA was district elections.

Voting Rights and Electoral Structure

Much of the research on cities and electoral structure suggests that at-large systems underrepresent blacks and Latinos (Davidson and Korbel 1981; Engstrom and McDonald 1981; Karnig and Welch 1980). There is also a "revisionist" position, which contends that at-large elections no longer adversely affect minority representation (Bullock and MacManus 1990). A comprehensive study utilizing 1981 data found that "Ward nomination in either nomination or election increases black council membership. . . . Black membership is higher when at least some councilors are elected by ward. . . . Hispanic 'underrepresentation,' while more severe than that of blacks is relatively insensitive to changes in election methods" (Zax 1990, 354).

Recent studies of this issue continue to contribute to our knowledge. Welch (1990), examining cities over 50,000 population, finds that at-large elections represent blacks better now than a decade ago, although district systems continue to enhance black representation more than at-large structures. Her data concerning the impact of electoral structure on Latinos are less conclusive. Bullock and MacManus (1990, 674) report a study that focused on Hispanic representation in cities over 25,000 population and found "a sizeable discount for all districting schemes in the rate at which Hispanic population translates into Hispanic-held council seats." However, single-member districts provide the least discount—in other words, single-member districts provide better representation for Hispanics in cities between 5 percent Hispanic and 50 percent Hispanic (Bullock and MacManus 1990, 674).

The debate often has been couched in terms of which electoral system enhances minority representation; this is certainly not an irrelevant question. We believe, however, that the electoral system should not be the sole focus, but that it should be viewed as an interactive measure whose effect may be less a function of a direct relationship between structure and minority representation and more a function of how the structure interacts with other variables to affect the ability of the minority community to obtain representation in the councils of government.[2]

This ongoing debate is important. The concept of representation is quite complex, and the inquiry into the relationship between electoral structure and minority representation has significant practical consequences for those communities involved in voting rights litigation.

Data and Methods

Welch used contemporary data from 314 U.S. cities of 50,000 and more population. Bullock and MacManus used data from a survey of 946 cities of over 25,000 population. We extend these studies by including smaller cities. We surveyed all Texas cities of over 20,000 population and included a one-out-of-four sample (randomly drawn) of cities between 2,500 and 20,000 population. Our study focuses on Mexican Americans rather than on the general Latino population. Given the theoretical importance of residential segregation to representation and the success of forms of electoral structure as discussed above, we include a measure of residential segregation in our aggregate analysis (Lopez 1981; Zax 1990).

We collected the data in January and February 1991. A total of 132 cities responded, for a response rate of 83 percent. Our survey instrument included the usual questions concerning electoral structure, size of city council, and ethnic composition of the council. In addition, if the respondent city utilized district or mixed elections, we asked when it had adopted that system and whether such change was in response to voting rights litigation. We are interested in what effect, if any, distance from the initial change to districted systems has on minority representation. Welch refers to, but does not find, the possibility that "voter hostility" toward a change of electoral systems might explain poor Hispanic representation in at-large seats within mixed systems (Welch 1990, 1065). We are also interested in what effect, if any, litigation has on the drawing of the districts. It may be that cities that voluntarily district may draw districts that are not as safe for minority candidates as would be those drawn as a result of litigation. On the other hand, it may also be that, to avoid litigation, cities that voluntarily change to districts first reach agreement on the composition of the districts with the potential plaintiffs. In the latter case, the districts would be essentially the same as those that had been litigated. Our anecdotal evidence supports the latter alternative.

A description of our sample cities may be useful. Minority representation is more prevalent in districted cities than in cities with at-large or mixed electoral systems. Seventy-nine percent of the at-large cities have no black council members, and 61 percent have no Mexican Americans on the council. Cities with mixed electoral systems are more likely than at-large cities to have minority representation. Of the twenty-four cities with mixed systems in our sample, 55 percent have black representatives and almost 60 percent have Mexican American representatives. We note that only 10 percent of the at-large seats within the mixed systems are held by Mexican Americans. This is not surprising. Within mixed systems, Mexican Americans seek office primarily in the districted contests and avoid the at-large seats where they will be at essentially the same disadvantage that they faced prior to the change to a mixed system. In effect, a mixed system is another form of a district system when one considers the efficacy of minority candidacies (Polinard, Wrinkle, and Longoria 1991). Consequently, in the following analyses we have treated districted and mixed systems as districted systems. Over three-fourths of our districted cities have Mexican American representatives and 56 percent have black representatives.

The average number of black and Mexican American representatives for all three types of systems is less than two; districted systems slightly exceed this average.

Table 3.1

Percentage of Mexican American City Council as a Function of Mexican American Population

Independent Variable	b	Standard Error
Mexican American population	0.986***	0.044

R^2 (adj.) = 0.79; F = 494, significance < 0.000; intercept = −3.96.
*** $p < 0.000$.

Table 3.2

Mexican American Percentage of City Council Members as a Function of Mexican American Political Resources

Independent Variable	b	Standard Error
% population Mexican American	0.971***	0.048
City population	−0.0001	0.0001
Mexican American–Anglo income ratio	0.171	0.158
At-large system	−0.871	3.155
Ward system	0.426	4.033
Size of city council	−0.561	1.171
Mexican American–Anglo residential segregation	0.097	0.113

R^2 (adj.) = 0.78; F = 69.3, significance = 0.000; intercept = −16.32.
*** $p < 0.000$.

We utilize regression to analyze the link between electoral structure and minority representation. We regress the percentage of the city council that is Mexican American on the percentage of the city population that is Mexican American.

Table 3.1 reports these results. There is a very strong and statistically significant relationship. Considering population alone, Mexican Americans get about 95 percent of the seats to which their proportion of the population would entitle them; this is a very strong finding. To further examine the impact of population on the percentage of city council seats that are held by Mexican Americans, we estimated an equation using form of electoral structure, Anglo–Mexican American income ratio, size of the city council, total population size of the city, and the Mexican American–Anglo residential segregation index discussed above. The results are shown in Table 3.2. As can be seen in the table, no variable other than percentage of the population that is

Table 3.3

Mexican American Percentage of City Council Members as a Function of Mexican American Political Resources
(without Mexican American population)

Independent Variable	b	Standard Error
City population	0.0000	0.0000
Mexican American–Anglo income ratio	0.955**	0.313
At-large system	5.310	6.399
Ward system	5.540	8.203
Size of city council	-3.891	2.273
Mexican American–Anglo residential segregation	0.703**	0.223

R^2 (adj.) = 0.10; F = 3.6, significance = 0.002; intercept = −1.92.
** $p < 0.01$.

Mexican American is statistically significant. In other words, the independent variable of Mexican American population percentage is the only traditional resource variable that makes a difference in the percentage of Mexican Americans occupying city council seats. This finding differs from Welch (1990, 1067), who found Hispanics were represented at a much lower rate than their population percentage.

We also explored the relative impact of the traditional political resources variables other than population percentage on Mexican American city council seats. To do this, we estimated another equation, omitting the percentage of the population that is Mexican American. The results are presented in Table 3.3. The resultant equation is significant, but the percentage of variation explained is quite small—about 10 percent. Two variables emerge as significant: the Mexican American–Anglo income ratio and the Mexican American–Anglo residential segregation index. Thus, in the absence of the percentage of the population that is Mexican American, these two variables are the significant predictors of Mexican American success in city council races.

We also examined the interactive effect between Anglo–Mexican American residential segregation and the percentage of the population that is Mexican American. We included this interactive term in an equation along with form of election structure, population, and Mexican American–Anglo income ratio. Table 3.4 reports the results. Here we see that the interactive term is positive and significant. Thus, as the

Table 3.4

Mexican American Percentage of City Council Members as a Function of Mexican American Political Resources with Interactive Terms

Independent Variable	b	Standard Error
City population	0.0000	0.0000
Mexican American–Anglo income ratio	0.221	0.179
At-large system	1.638	3.498
Ward system	0.906	4.730
Size of city council	−0.00005***	0.00001
Population interaction with residential segregation	0.0270***	0.001

R^2 (adj.) = 0.71; F = 52.4, significance = 0.000; intercept = −13.51.
*** $p < 0.000$.

percentage of Mexican Americans in the population increases, and as residential segregation becomes more pronounced, the percentage of Mexican Americans on the city council also increases. There also is a weak relationship between the size of the city council and the percentage of Mexican American representation. This lends soft support to Taebel's (1978) analysis.

In examining the conditional effect of varying Mexican American populations across the two electoral types, we construct dummy and interaction variables in the following equation:

$$PMACC = b_1 \text{Ward} + b_2 \text{ At-large} + b_3 \text{ Ward} \times MAPOP + b_4 \text{ At-large} \times MAPOP + b_5 \text{ Memcc} + b_6 \text{ Popsize} + e;$$

where Ward = 1 if the city uses only district elections, 0 otherwise; At-large = 1 if the city uses only at-large elections, otherwise = 0; Ward*$MAPOP$ is an interactive term multiplying the dummy x percentage Mexican American population; At-large x $MAPOP$ is an interactive term multiplying the dummy times the Mexican American percentage of the population; Memcc = the number of members on the city council; Popsize = the 1990 city population.

We estimate one equation, suppressing the intercept, which allows us to examine both types of electoral structures and the interactive terms in one equation (Meier and Stewart 1991).[3]

Table 3.5

Mexican American Percentage of City Council Members as a Function of Mexican American Political Resources with Interactive Terms: All Cities

Independent Variable	b	Standard Error
City population	−0.738	1.30
At-large slope	1.03***	0.053
Ward slope	0.820***	0.101
Size of city council	0.171	1.20
At-large intercept	−9.03	7.57
Ward intercept	−4.56	8.53

R^2 (adj.) = 0.83; F = 98.14, significance = 0.000.
*** $p < 0.000$.

Table 3.5 presents the results of the equation. The results, in general, support Welch's findings (1990). We see that both systems have negative intercepts, which are not statistically significant. At-large systems have the largest negative intercept (−9.03) and a slope of 1.03, which is statistically significant. It indicates that, once the threshold of Mexican American population is reached, at-large systems represent Mexican Americans slightly better than districted systems. There is little surprise here, since at-large systems would be expected to be most responsive to larger numbers. The districted systems have a negative intercept of 4.56 and a statistically significant slope of 0.820. None of the other independent variables was significant.

We believed it was possible that at-large cities with small Mexican American populations and little residential segregation plus at-large cities with very large (60 percent plus) Mexican American populations might mask the effect of electoral structure. Consequently, we constructed an equation looking at a subset of our sample composed of those cities with high residential segregation (0.30 or greater) and Mexican American populations of less than 50 percent. Table 3.6 reports these results. As expected, we find that, in this context, districted systems are a significant predictor of Mexican American representation, with a slope of 0.45. At-large systems were not statistically significant. It is clear that a high degree of residential segregation combined with less than 50 percent Mexican American population enhances Mexican American representation on city councils.

Table 3.6

Mexican American Percentage of City Council Members as a Function of Mexican American Political Resources with Interactive Terms: Subset Cities

Independent Variable	b	Standard Error
City population	0.0001	0.0002
At-large slope	0.3608	0.260
Ward slope	0.450*	0.195
Size of city council	0.531	2.07
At-large intercept	−3.358	11.5
Ward intercept	−0.8078	12.9

R^2 (adj.) = 0.77; F = 5.7, significance = 0.000.
* $p < 0.05$.

Discussion

We find, as did Welch, that the differences between district and at-large election systems are not as well-defined as earlier studies suggest. Although the differences may be small, district elections continue to offer the friendliest environments to Mexican American representation. We expected the differences to be more marked, but, as discussed above, the inclusion of a large number of at-large cities with small Mexican American populations and little residential segregation, and of at-large cities with very large Mexican American populations may be masking some of the impact of structure.[4]

We note again that it may be misleading to cast the current debate in terms of which form of electoral system drives Mexican American representation. Rather, we should recognize that the form of electoral system is an interactive variable, serving to enhance or depress minority representation given the presence of such other variables as residential segregation, percentage of minority population, and income ratios.

Conclusions

In the main, conventional wisdom continues to be served. Where Mexican American population percentages are low, districted systems offer a better chance of representation than do at-large systems. The differences between the systems are not as distinct as we had expected, but we anticipate that the addition of residential segregation data currently being collected will result in enhanced discrimination between the systems (Vedlitz and Johnson 1982; Zax 1990).

In addition, the fact that Mexican American representation in the mixed systems continues to be primarily in the districted portion of the system suggests that enhancement of Mexican American representation in these systems might come from the adoption of alternative forms of electoral structure for the at-large seats.[5] For example, cumulative voting might produce increased Mexican American representation in mixed or at-large systems (see Engstrom, Taebel, and Cole 1989).

Notes

1. Our use of the history and development of LULAC is based on the work of San Miguel (1987) and Allsup (1977).

2. We are indebted to Professor Richard Engstrom for this observation.

3. Because the R^2 term in an equation in which the intercept has been surpressed is not accurate, we estimate a second equation and the R^2 term from that equation (Meier and Stewart 1991).

4. We found no statistically significant relationship between the distance from the time of change to districted systems, nor was there a relationship between representation and whether a district or mixed system had occurred in response to litigation.

5. Again, we thank Professor Richard Engstrom for his insights on this point.

4

Electoral Structure and City Council Member Attitudes

The attitudes and behavior of local policy makers constitute an area of long-standing concern to political scientists. Decisions made at the city council level have far-reaching consequences. Indeed, for most Americans, decisions made at city hall tend to affect their lives more directly than decisions made in Washington, D.C.

The urban reform movement had a major impact on a wide range of issues relating to these "small, natural state legislative groups" (Loveridge 1971, viii). We are interested in such issues as the demographics of councilpersons, the impact of electoral structure on the recruitment of city councilpersons, the impact of electoral structure on the relationships within the council, the mode of representation practiced by council members, and the distinctive policy orientations held by these legislators.

The recent work by Welch and Bledsoe, *Urban Reform and Its Consequences: A Study in Representation* (1988), both complements and extends earlier works in this research area such as Heilig and Mundt, *Your Voice at City Hall* (1984), and Browning, Marshall, and Tabb, *Protest Is Not Enough* (1984). Among the major points of concern in all of these works is the impact of electoral structure on urban institutions and policy as well as urban representation. As Welch and Bledsoe note,

> [C]rucial issues of democratic representation were subsumed under seemingly more mundane issues of whether city council members should be elected on partisan or nonpartisan ballots, or by wards or in the city as a whole. . . . These questions have clear relevance to public policy. (1988, xiii–xiv)

This chapter focuses on these concerns. While the previous chapter provided a macro-level analysis of Texas cities, this chapter, by examining the responses of mayors and council members, provides a micro-level look.

Chief among these concerns are the nature and style of representation.[1] In a discussion about representation, it is common to distinguish between active and passive representation. Pitkin (1967, 67) refers to "descriptive representation," that is, she defines representation in terms of the characteristics of the representatives as passive representation where the emphasis is on "being something rather than doing something." This contrasts with active representation, where the representative engages in activity on behalf of the represented. Meier and Stewart (1991, 87) suggest that implicit in the concept of passive representation is the idea that other forms of representation will follow. Electing a minority candidate to office (passive representation) may well spur the development of other forms of representation.

Once a minority legislator has been elected to office, passive representation has been achieved. Actual policy change or impact, however, has not. The linkage between passive representation and actually doing something for the minority group (active representation) generally has been conceptualized in two ways: electorally and in terms of representative bureaucracy, that is, the socialization process (Meier and Stewart 1991). As one political commentator put it,

> For representative government to work, the politicians elected to office have to be concerned about the priorities of the people they represent. Or, they have to be afraid of political fallout from voters' outrage. (Stinson 1993)

Concern about the priorities of the people they represent can be thought of as part of the representative bureaucracy component, wherein elected officials share the same background, attitudes, and priorities as those whom they represent (Mosher 1968; Meier and Stewart 1991).

The strong bond of socialization that race and ethnicity create helps to strengthen the linkage between passive and active representation for minority legislators. Recent research has documented the strong impact of ethnicity, particularly that of Hispanics (de la Garza et al. 1992; de la Garza and Weaver 1983; Garcia et al. 1992; Keefe and Padilla 1987). De la Garza and Weaver have identified the distinctive role that leads Mexican Americans to differ from Anglos in issue priorities. They note that, "on local issues, Anglos and Chicanos have distinct priorities" (de la Garza and Weaver 1983, 25). De la Garza et al. (1991) have identified the strong impact that ethnicity has in regard to immigration issues. Ethnicity becomes particularly salient when a co-ethnic is seeking election or when national origin issues are particularly salient in the campaign or discussion (Garcia et al. 1992, 17). As de la Garza and Weaver put it,

> [I]t seems clear that there are coherent and distinct Chicano and Anglo electorates, but their existence becomes manifest only on those issues which tap the long-standing divisions between the two groups. Thus, on explicit racial issues or social welfare, the existence of the two groups is clear. On issues such as energy, crime, defense and the environment, the boundaries dissipate and ethnicity has little effect on policy orientations. (1983, 26–27)

This leads us to suggest that, especially for Mexican American legislators and bureaucrats, ethnicity can be and often is especially salient in regard to how legislators and/or bureaucrats defines their representational role. This should be especially true for those policy makers who represent minority districts or communities or who define a minority neighborhood as one of their primary constituencies.

The electoral connection between passive and active representation also has some merit. There is a well-established literature that suggests that reelection concerns are primary motivations of legislators (Fiorina 1977; Yiannakis 1981). The emphasis upon electoral structure, particularly some form of district elections, also contributes to the strength of the electoral argument, especially in reference to the minority community. One of the assumptions of district election systems, an assumption warranted by most research on the issue, is that minority voters will be able to elect a candidate of their choice. For many elected officials, however, there are substantial reasons to doubt the efficacy of the electoral connection alone (McCrone and Stone 1986, 957). McCrone and Stone say, "There is ample evidence that citizens will not regularly force their elected representatives to conform to their policy preferences" (1986, 956). Baron notes that, "Representation . . . is an endogenous function of both institutional structure . . . and the strategies adopted by parties and voters in the context of that institutional structure" (1993, 34). A lack of information on the part of both representative and constituents often limits the connection, as does the overwhelming tendency of incumbents to win reelection. Simply put, many incumbents either do not have any opposition or do not have a viable opponent (Meier and Stewart 1991, 88; Prewitt 1970). In such a context, representatives are much freer to pursue their own agenda rather than that of their constituency.

These two perspectives are not as separate and distinct as they might appear. Those minority representatives who share the issue agenda and concerns of their constituents (the socialization perspective) have a strong incentive to keep the electoral connection strong so as to allow them to continue to serve. Clingermayer and Feiock put it this way: "This model presumes that council members are reelection-seeking and therefore quite interested in the demands of their constituencies" (1993, 200). In addition, those representatives with progressive political ambitions have an added incentive to maintain a close electoral connection with the home folks. Not only will they seek reelection, but they need to build a solid base for advancement to higher political office.

Methodology

Our data are from a survey of council members of all Texas cities over 20,000 population and a one-in-four random sample of Texas cities between 2,500 and 20,000 population. By including all cities between 20,000 and 50,000 population as well as a sample of smaller cities, this study expands and extends the bulk of the literature. Councilpersons from 175 cities were asked to take part in the survey; we conducted a follow-up mailing to those who had not responded to our first request. A total of 672 usable responses were obtained, for a responses rate of 56 percent. The survey instrument was modeled after the one used by Welch and Bledsoe in their 1988 study, thus affording us comparability with the most recent national study.[2]

Welch and Bledsoe (1988, 20) found a slightly higher tendency to respond to the survey among at-large council members than among those elected by district, as well as "a decline in the quality of responses in later stages of sampling." Our respondents displayed no such tendency. We compared the means of the two waves of our sample on a number of socioeconomic dimensions, including age, ethnicity, education, and income, and found no significant differences between the first and second wave. Unlike Welch and Bledsoe, we found that those responses that were mailed later were as complete as the earlier ones in terms of responses to the open-ended items.

We did find an underrepresentation of minority council members in the survey. We know from the responses of city clerks that council membership of the sample Texas cities includes 177 Hispanic members, or 14.6 percent of the entire number of council members. The response from Hispanic council members totaled only 5.8 percent of the sample. Given this underrepresentation, we decided to reweight the sample to obtain more accurate population estimates.[3]

In addition to simple descriptive summaries, we use two basic forms of analysis. One is the OLS regression, the most widely used analytical technique in social science (Welch and Bledsoe 1988, 21). This technique requires that the dependent variable be in a continuous form. However, because several of the dependent variables that we utilize range from 0 to 1, OLS regression is not appropriate. The appropriate form of analysis in these cases is logistic regression (logit) producing an equation by which we can estimate the probabilities of support for the dependent variable (Aldrich and Nelson 1984; Agresti 1984). This procedure allows us to estimate the relative strength or effect that the different types of variables have on our dependent variable. As Cleary and Angel note, a major appeal of the general linear model is the direct interpretation of coefficients. OLS coefficients are interpretable as the change in the dependent variable associated with a unit change in the independent variable, holding the values of the other independent variables constant (Cleary and Angel 1984, 336). Logistic regression does not allow such an interpretation because of the assumption of a difference in the underlying relationship (Erikson, Lancaster, and Romero 1989, 340). However, the procedure does allow us to estimate the probability of support in a number of different circumstances.

Who Are the Council Members?

The National League of Cities study found slightly more than 26 percent of council members were female; approximately 13 percent were minority, with most minorities elected by district (Svara 1991, 14). Other demographic features of city council members nationally include high education levels: 30 percent with a college degree and an additional 37 percent with a graduate or advanced degree. At-large council members tend to be slightly older: 29 percent are over fifty, compared with 25 percent for district council members (Svara 1991, 16).

The council members in our study are described in Table 4.1, which shows that they are well educated, with almost two-thirds having either a college or postgraduate degree. Most council members are in professional or managerial occupations. Their income also is fairly high, with only 15 percent reporting incomes under $35,000 and 46 percent reporting incomes of $65,000 or more. The average age is 51 years and the average length of time lived in the community is 28 years. Males outnumber women, 82 percent to 18 percent, a fairly common finding for local legislators (Welch and Bledsoe 1988). Our data support Welch and Bledsoe's finding that women are more likely to be found on city councils in the larger cities.

Council members have served an average of 4.6 years on the city council. This is generally in line with Welch and Bledsoe (1988). Sixty-four percent of the council members identify themselves as moderate to very conservative, 24 percent say they are middle-of-the-road, and only 12 percent are liberal.

City council members do not aspire to higher office—few consider the city council important as a stepping-stone to higher political office. Welch and Bledsoe (1988, 26) report that 30 percent of their national study indicated that the possibility of seeking higher office was important in their decision to serve on the city council. Only 14 percent of our sample reported that this was the case.

In general, then, this is the "snapshot" of the city council members. By and large it conforms to the findings of the Welch and Bledsoe national study as well as those of the National League of Cities study (Svara 1991). However, when we distinguish between Anglo and Mexican American council respondents, some interesting divergences occur. The Mexican American council member is younger, 44 years of age, and less well educated—51 percent have no college degree. In terms of gender, Mexican American females are slightly better represented than are Anglo females. Mexican American council members also are more conservative than their Anglo counterparts, with 70 percent describing themselves as conservative and only 9 percent as liberal. Although younger, Mexican American council members tend to report living in the community longer. They have served, on average, only three years on the council, with only 20 percent serving six years or more. In terms of political ambitions, 25 percent of the Mexican

Table 4.1

Descriptive Information on Council Members

Gender:	
Male	82%
Female	18
Income:	
< $35,000	15%
$35,000–64,999	38
$65,000+	46
Occupation:	
Prof./mgr.	65%
Other	35
Education:	
High school	10%
Some college	28
College grad.	29
Prof./grad.	33
Ethnicity:	
Mexican American	16%
Anglo	84
Ideology:	
Conservative	64%
Moderate	24
Liberal	12
Average age	51
Years in community	28
Average size of council	7
Average years on council	4.6

American council members viewed service on the city council as a stepping-stone to higher office, substantially above the Anglo percentage.

Tenure, Gender, and Ideology

We now explore the relationship between electoral structure and the ethnicity and socioeconomic characteristics of elected city council members.[4] Table 4.2 reports the differences between council members by method of election. There are relatively few major differences. Anglos are slightly more likely to represent at-large districts, while

Table 4.2

Differences between Council Members Elected At-Large and by District

	At-Large	District
Gender:		
Male	81%	82%
Female	19	18
Income:		
< $35,000	16%	14%
$35,000–64,999	38	38
$65,000+	46	48
Occupation:		
Prof./mgr.	67%	60%
Other	33	40
Education:		
High school	10%	7%
Some college	27	30
College grad.	29	30
Prof./grad.	33	33
Ethnicity:		
Mexican American	14%	19%
Anglo	86	81
Ideology:		
Conservative	62%	64%
Moderate	24	25
Liberal	14	11
Average age	41	40.5
Years in community**	26.6	31.4
Average size of council	6.5	7.7
Average years on council***	4.9	4.1

**Mean of district significantly different from at-large at 0.01 level.
***Mean of district significantly different from at-large at 0.000 level.

Mexican Americans are slightly more likely to represent wards. The most significant differences come in the number of years in the community, with district council members more likely to have lived in their communities significantly longer than at-large representatives. And the district council members have served a significantly shorter tenure on the city council than at-large council members. Other than these factors, most differences reported are relatively minor. Welch and Bledsoe (1988, 50) found that district elections provided a greater opportunity for people of lower income and lower educational levels to be elected. That finding is not well supported by our data, which may well be because of our inclusion of smaller cities with more homogeneous populations. We found, as

did Welch and Bledsoe, that district council members were not significantly more likely to be liberal than at-large council members. Indeed,
our sample of district council members is somewhat more conservative
than the at-large members. There have been suggestions in the literature that women are more likely to be disadvantaged by district elections (Welch and Karnig 1979). Our data do not support this. There is
no significant difference in gender representation between the two
types of electoral systems. More significant differences are revealed in
the following sections on political ambition and policy representation.

Political Ambition and Political Support

We asked the council members why they initially decided to seek
election to the city council.[5] We also asked them to rate each of seven
items on a scale of importance. The potential reasons included responses that indicate strong issue concern, representational foci on
either the district as a whole or the representative's own neighborhood,
an indication of progressive political ambition, recruitment by a political party, and personal reasons, such as enjoying politics and increasing business contacts. The responses are presented in Table 4.3.

There are some important differences between district council members and at-large council members, but also some strong similarities.
Overwhelmingly, both district and at-large council members indicate
that serving the district as a whole is important (91 percent at-large, 97
percent district). More than half of each group indicated that enjoyment of politics and having a strong concern about some specific issue
were important. Neither group reported significant political ambitions.
The lack of political ambition among local policy makers is congruent
with the previous research that suggests that those at higher levels of
office—state rather than local—are more likely to be politically ambitious (Burt-Way and Kelly 1991, 15). These data also conform to the
results of Miller and Wrinkle (1984, 9), who found that less than
one-half of Texas council members held progressive political ambitions. However, they found that council members elected from at-large
systems were more likely to be politically ambitious than those elected
from districted systems (Miller and Wrinkle 1984, 9). Our data do not
support that finding: there is no significant difference between at-large
and district council members on seeking local office as a stepping-
stone to other political office.[6]

Table 4.3

Differences between Council Members Elected At-Large and by District on Reasons for Seeking Local Office (in %)

	Importance	At-Large	District
Because I was persuaded	No	81	91
by a political party organization.	Yes	19	9**
To serve my	No	21	13
neighborhood.	Yes	79	87*
As a stepping-stone to	No	88	84
other political office.	Yes	12	16
To serve the district as	No	9	3
a whole.	Yes	91	97
To increase business	No	84	87
contacts.	Yes	16	13
Because I enjoy politics.	No	38	34
	Yes	62	66
Because of a strong concern	No	37	40
I had about some specific issue.	Yes	63	60

*Mean of district significantly different from at-large at 0.05 level.
**Mean of district significantly different from at-large at 0.01 level.

However, two reasons for seeking local office do distinguish at-large and district council members. At-large representatives are significantly more likely to report that they were persuaded to seek office by a political party (19 percent) than district members (9 percent). More district representatives report that they ran for local office to "serve my neighborhood" than do at-large representatives (87 percent versus 79 percent). This recruitment difference is likely linked to the size of the electoral district. At-large representatives are elected citywide and, as a consequence, tend to have more expensive campaigns, thus requiring more resources. Apparently, a political party organization (even in Texas, where the local elections are nonpartisan) can serve as a gatekeeper for local candidates, or the elections are not really as nonpartisan as is claimed. Miller and Wrinkle (1984) found no significant difference between electoral forms in terms of political recruitment.

Table 4.4

Differences between Council Members Elected At-Large and by District on Support When Seeking Local Office (in %)

	Importance	At-Large	District
Political party	No	90	92
	Yes	10	8
Organized labor	No	94	88
	Yes	6	12
Business groups	No	42	38
	Yes	58	62
Neighborhood organizations	No	50	42
	Yes	50	58*
Racial or ethnic groups	No	84	82
	Yes	16	18
Single-issue group	No	77	82
	Yes	23	18

* Mean of district significantly different from at-large at 0.05 level.

Of particular interest is the clear distinction that motivates council members to run to "support my neighborhood." Although a sizable majority of both at-large and district council members reported that this was important, significantly more district council members said that it was important. This motivational focus blends with the representation focus discussed below. We would expect that council members who report this motivation for seeking office would tend to have an areal representational focus (see Clingermayer and Feiock 1993; Welch and Bledsoe 1988).

Motivation, in and of itself, is not sufficient to ensure election to local office. As Vogel notes, "A major factor influencing a candidate's decision to run for office is the availability of money to finance a campaign" (1992, 90). Also of importance are other significant resources such as volunteer workers and campaign organizers. In an attempt to ascertain the relative importance of various groups to the electoral campaign, we asked how important each of six different groups was in terms of support provided in the last campaign.[7] The results are found in Table 4.4.

Both at-large and district candidates report similar levels of importance for the six groups in the last election. Relatively high percentages of council members elected via both electoral forms indicate that support from business groups and neighborhood groups was important in the last campaign. This is not surprising, since both of these groups historically have been important in local election campaigns.

The relationship between recruitment and electoral support is an interesting one. At-large council members were more likely to report that political parties influenced their decision to seek office than were district council members. In terms of support for the election, however, both at-large and district council members overwhelmingly dismiss the importance of political parties. In a nonpartisan setting this would be expected. What may be happening here is that individuals known to be associated with a political party were involved in recruitment of at-large members to run, and then the necessary resources were provided by individuals and business groups.

Only one difference in terms of support for the last election between council members from the two electoral forms was statistically significant—that of support from neighborhood organizations. District council members were significantly more likely to report that such support was important in their campaign. Clingermayer and Feiock (1993, 200) suggest that council members who represent more diverse constituencies, such as at-large constituencies, are more likely to look to "organized interests that may provide them with resources that will increase their chances of political survival." Thus, it is not surprising that council members elected by districts would find neighborhood groups more important than do at-large representatives. What is more surprising is that there is so much unanimity as to importance of support from the other groups.

Mexican Americans and Political Support

We also examined the motivations for seeking office by ethnicity. We expected that Mexican American council members would tend to have different motivations than Anglo council members have, and that within the Mexican American community, there would be differences between those elected by district and those Mexican American council members elected at-large.

The socioeconomic differences between Mexican Americans and

Table 4.5

**Differences between Anglo and Mexican American Council Members on
Reasons for Seeking Local Office** (in %)

	Importance	Anglo	Mexican American
Because I was persuaded	No	88	81
by a political party organization.	Yes	12	19
To serve my	No	19	14
neighborhood.	Yes	81	86
As a stepping-stone to	No	88	79*
other political office.	Yes	12	21
To serve the district as	No	6	12
a whole.	Yes	94	88
To increase business	No	86	78**
contacts.	Yes	14	22
Because I enjoy politics.	No	37	38
	Yes	63	62
Because of a strong concern	No	40	30**
I had about some specific issue.	Yes	60	70

*Mean of Mexican Americans significantly different from Anglos at 0.05 level.
**Mean of Mexican Americans significantly different from Anglos at 0.01 level.

Anglos in terms of reasons for seeking local elective office and the importance of support from various groups when running are reported in Tables 4.5 and 4.6.

Mexican Americans and Anglos report similar reasons for seeking local office, with three significant differences. Mexican Americans and Anglos differed significantly in terms of running to increase business contacts, as a stepping-stone to other political office, and because of a strong concern about some specific issue. More Mexican Americans reported running for reasons of political ambition (21 percent versus 12 percent), to increase business contacts (22 percent versus 14 percent), and for a specific concern (70 percent versus 60 percent). These findings portray a more ambitious, business-oriented minority policy maker than conventional wisdom describes.

Mexican Americans and Anglos differ significantly on the impor-

Table 4.6

Differences between Anglo and Mexican American Council Members on Support When Seeking Local Office (in %)

	Importance	Anglo	Mexican American
Political party	No	94	71
	Yes	6	29***
Organized labor	No	96	72
	Yes	4	28***
Business groups	No	42	33
	Yes	58	67
Neighborhood organizations	No	53	28
	Yes	47	72***
Racial or ethnic groups	No	89	61
	Yes	11	39***
Single-issue group	No	80	74
	Yes	20	26

***Mean of Mexican Americans significantly different from Anglos at 0.000 level.

tance of support from four of the six groups listed. Mexican Americans are more likely than Anglos to report that support from political parties was important (29 percent versus 6 percent), that support from organized labor was important (28 percent versus 4 percent), that support from neighborhood groups was important (72 percent versus 47 percent), and that support from racial or ethnic groups was important (39 percent versus 11 percent). Welch and Bledsoe (1988, 52) found that district-based elections reinforce the clout of racial and neighborhood groups and may serve to balance the political system. Since almost two out of every three Mexican American council members are elected from districts, it is not surprising that racial/ethnic groups and neighborhood organizations were important to Mexican Americans in their elections. What is somewhat surprising is the difference in the degree of importance: less than one-third of Mexican Americans reported them as important, because of their attachment to political parties and organized labor between Mexican Americans and Anglos. It may well be that Mexican Americans, lacking the resources of Anglo candidates, turned to a more diverse set of groups for support in their electoral bids (e.g., Clingermayer and Feiock 1993; Welch and Bledsoe 1988).

In an attempt to explain more fully the importance of various reasons for seeking local elective office, we estimated a logistic regression equation on all six of the reasons given, with form of election, ethnicity, size of city, ideology of the council member, previous political activity of the council member, and the council member's view of constituent interests as independent. The logistic regression allowed us to assess the relative significance of each of these independent variables, taken as a whole, thus expanding the bivariate analyses discussed above. The results of the logistic regression are reported in Table 4.7.

Table 4.7 reports only four regressions. These were the only significant equations. The four significant equations correctly classify an impressive percentage of cases and have highly significant model chi-squares. We found some expected relationships: ethnicity is significant in three equations, form of election and previous political activity in two equations, and ideology in only one. Size of the city and council members' perceptions of their constituents' interests are not significant in any equation.

Being Mexican American contributes to identifying serving neighborhood and increasing business contacts as important reasons for seeking elective office. Anglo council members report serving the entire district as an important factor in seeking elective office.

District council members report serving the whole district as important, while at-large council members note the importance of political parties and increasing business contacts as important reasons for seeking office. Those persons without prior political experience report being persuaded to run by a political party organization as an important reason to seek office. Persons with prior political experience report a motivation to serve the district as a whole as important.

In brief, local office holders report a variety of motivations for seeking office distinguished by their ethnicity, method of election, and prior political activity.

Representational Styles

The nature of the representational style adopted by policy makers has long interested political scientists. As Welch and Bledsoe (1988) note,

Table 4.7

Logistic Regression of Importance of Reasons for Seeking Local Office

Independent Variables	Political Party	Serve Neighborhood	Serve Whole District	Increase Business Contacts
Form of election	-0.91** (0.32)	0.16 (0.28)	1.17* (0.52)	-0.40 (0.29)
Ethnicity	0.35 (0.32)	0.65* (0.32)	-0.78* (0.39)	0.83** (0.32)
City population	-0.54 (0.43)	0.52 (0.32)	0.43 (0.62)	0.35 (0.33)
Previous political activity	-0.52* (0.24)	0.86** (0.26)	-0.17 (0.33)	0.03 (0.14)
Ideology	-0.04 (0.25)	-0.18 (0.28)	-0.57 (0.35)	-0.93** (0.30)
Constituent interests	-0.47 (0.24)	0.28 (0.29)	0.19 (0.35)	-0.40 (0.26)
Intercept	-0.91	-2.77	2.65	-1.34
% correctly classified	84.0	86.7	92.9	85.6
Model chi-square	23.1	23.8	18.3	18.3
DF	6	6	6	6
Significance	$p < 0.000$	$p < 0.000$	$p < 0.005$	$p < 0.005$

Standard errors in parentheses.
*$p < 0.05$ level.
**$p < 0.01$ level.

the primary focus has been on areal representation—the focus of a representative's district as opposed to the city as a whole. Clingermayer and Feiock (1993) discuss this in terms of the homogeneity (or lack thereof) of the representative's district. They argue that the representatives of homogeneous constituencies tend to be responsive to "territorial groups" such as neighborhood organizations, homeowners' associations, and unorganized interests and individuals (Clingermayer and Feiock 1993, 201). Representatives of more diverse communities (such as an entire city) should be more attentive to groups that have less clear-cut territorial interests. Such groups might include growth and development interests, unions, and other citywide interests

(Clingermayer and Feiock 1993, 201). Following that line of thought, we expect that representatives elected by district would tend to have the territorial focus while at-large representatives would tend to have the citywide focus.

Welch and Bledsoe identified expected differences between at-large and district-elected representatives:

> Those elected at-large will be more likely than those elected by district to believe that they "represent the city as a whole"; those elected by district will be more likely to see themselves representing neighborhood or ethnic constituencies. We might expect at-large representatives to be more likely to feel they represent business constituencies, those elected by district labor constituencies. (1988, 59)

We asked council members to assess the relative importance that they attach to representing different constituencies.[8] Welch and Bledsoe found remarkably little variation in response. Our data, reported in Table 4.8, support the findings of Welch and Bledsoe.

Sixty-five percent of the respondents said that representation of racial or ethnic groups was not very important, 85 percent said the same for representing a partisan or ideological group, and 78 percent said that representing a labor union was not very important. While the overall responses indicated little variation, when we controlled for ethnicity and form of election, significant differences did emerge. Mexican Americans significantly differed from Anglos on every representational measure. And, council members elected by district differed significantly from those elected at-large on five of the representational measures. As expected, Mexican Americans were more likely to report a territorial focus, but interestingly, so were those elected at-large. This latter finding was not expected, and is confounding. As expected, both Mexican Americans and those elected by district tended to say that representation of a racial or ethnic group was important. Mexican Americans also were significantly more likely to say that representation of a business interest was important.

To understand the pattern of representational foci more fully, we performed a correlational analysis and a factor analysis on these data. The findings are reported in Table 4.9.

As expected, the largest correlation is that of race and neighborhood, a positive 0.44. The largest negative relationship is that of

Table 4.8

**Differences between Anglo and Mexican American
Council Members and between At-Large and District Elections on
Representational Foci** (in %)

	Importance	Anglo	Mexican American	District	At-Large
Organized labor	No	98	91	94	98
	Yes	2	9***	6	2##
Business groups	No	92	79***	90	91
	Yes	8	21	10	9
Neighborhood organizations	No	76	38	50	80###
	Yes	24	62***	50	20
Racial or ethnic groups	No	93	58	78	90
	Yes	7	42***	22	10#
Single-issue group	No	96	90	92	95
	Yes	4	10**	8	5#

**Mean of Mexican Americans significantly different from Anglos at 0.01 level.
***Mean of Mexican Americans significantly different from Anglos at 0.000 level.
#Mean of district council members significantly different from at-large council members at 0.05 level.
##Mean of district council members significantly different from at-large council members at 0.01 level.
###Mean of district council members significantly different from at-large council members at 0.000 level.

neighborhood and city as a whole, −0.09. We found a positive relationship between business and neighborhood foci where a negative one had been expected. We also found a clustering of business, labor, single-interest, and racial/ethnic foci, intercorrelated at the 0.16 to 0.41 level. The city as a whole focus is distinguished from other representational foci. In essence, there appears to be some degree of conflict in representing the city as a whole and other representational foci (see Welch and Bledsoe 1988, 63). The negative correlations between city as a whole and five of the other six representational areas would seem to indicate that this representational focus is somewhat different from other foci. The size and direction of these findings parallel Welch and Bledsoe (1988, 62). Texas council members share similar representational foci with those of their colleagues across the nation.

Table 4.9

Various Representational Foci

(A) Intercorrelations

Subject	Neighbor-hood	City	Ideology	Business	Single Interest	Race
Neighborhood	−.09	0.15	0.21	0.15	0.44	0.21
City		−.05	0.04	−0.01	−0.07	−0.04
Ideology			0.21	0.31	0.25	0.32
Business				0.16	0.26	0.39
Single interest					0.19	0.41
Race						0.28
Labor						

(B) Factor Analysis

Foci	Factor I Group Focus	Factor II Areal Foci
Labor	0.77	0.11
Single interest	0.73	−0.10
Ideology	0.63	0.10
Business	0.54	0.24
Neighborhood	0.23	0.74
Race/ethnic	0.37	0.67
City as a whole	0.18	−0.57
Eigenvalue	2.34	1.11
Percentage of variation explained	33.5	15.9

The factor analysis is presented in Table 4.9(B). Two factors emerged: a groups focus factor and an areal focus factor. These two factors indicate two clusters of representational foci. The groups focus factor has four foci that load; it explains almost 34 percent of the variation. The second factor—the areal factor—has two positive loadings from what Clingermayer and Feiock might call territorial groups and one negative focus—the city as a whole. This second factor explains about 16 percent of the variation. These analyses mirror those of Welch and Bledsoe, except that in their analysis three factors emerged—the third one was a partisan factor. Our data, in nonpartisan Texas, do not support this third factor. Again, it is significant to note the negative loading of the city as a whole focus with the two other components of the areal focus. It is quite clear that there is some degree of conflict in representing the city as a whole and other representational foci. Note that one major linchpin of the urban reform ideology—areal representation—with the city as a whole focus is distinguished from the other representational foci. By adopting representational foci other than those of traditional urban reform ideology, Texas council members seem to have moved away from that ideological position. The bivariate analyses indicate that election structure and ethnicity are primary emphases on altering the traditional reform position.

Representation and Council Member Behavior

Our analyses clearly demonstrate that council members maintain two distinct clusters of representational foci. Given this duality of representational foci, what is to be expected in terms of council member behavior? Clingermayer and Feiock say, "Differences in the interests that are represented should also entail differences in the issues with which city legislators choose to involve themselves and the stances that they take toward those issues" (1993, 201).

One of the major functions of any elected representative is what Eulau and Karps (1978, 62) define as service responsiveness. Many studies have focused on service responsiveness, especially at the national or state level, including those of Brown, Fuchs, and Hoadley (1979), Cain, Ferejohn, and Fiorina (1979), and McAdams (1980). In fact, as Fowler, Stonecash, and Carrothers put it, "The essential ingredient of the 'political establishment' is constituency service, which binds voters, politicians and bureaucrats in a self-interested relationship" (1982, 3). Representatives, from members of Congress to members of city and town councils, are called upon by their constituents for a staggering variety of tasks, including personal favors. Members of Congress, as well as some of the state representatives, have staff members devoted to this effort. This is not typically the case with city council members, who often have little or no staff and have to respond to constituent demands themselves (Welch and Bledsoe 1988, 68). Greene (1981) notes that council members often are the first government officials contacted by citizens with some form of service demand. Peterson and Dutton (1981, 8) argue that constituency service activities—what they call errand boy behavior—are associated with lack of wealth in a constituency. Representatives from poor constituencies engage in more errand boy behavior. In a study of the five Southwestern states, Wrinkle and Miller (1984) found that council size and council member ethnicity were the best predictors of constituency service. Apparently, council members from large councils with sizable minority populations respond with increased constituency service. Following Black's (1972) suggestion that electoral competition will increase council member behavior aimed at ensuring reelection, several scholars have attempted to document a relationship between electoral competition and high levels of constituency service. However, the findings of Dutton (1975), Greene (1981), and Bledsoe and Welch (1983) do not support this contention.

We asked respondents to indicate how many hours per week they spent on city business and how much of that time was spent on constituency service activities.[9] The council members in our survey spend approximately fifteen hours a week on city business and 56 percent of that time on constituency service. However, there are significant differences in terms of ethnicity and form of election in relation to the time spent by council members. Anglo council members spend an average of ten-plus hours a week on city council business and approximately 48 percent of that time on constituency service. Mexican American council members spend an average of twenty-one hours a week on city business and 71 percent of that time on constituency service. Council members elected by district spend approximately eighteen hours a week on city business and 77 percent of that time on constituency service, while at-large council members spend only fourteen hours per week on city business and approximately 47 percent of that time on constituency service. Thus, it is clear that there are significant differences in terms of both ethnicity and form of election regarding how much time council members devote to city business and how they spend their time.

What these bivariate analyses do not explain for us is the more complicated interrelationships that help to explain constituency service by council members. Welch and Bledsoe (1988, 69–75) provide an excellent model of constituency service. They argue that one must take into account "a complex set of relationships between the city environment, the election structure and its impact on the membership of the council, and the predisposition to do constituency service" (1988, 69). Their analyses suggest several important factors for consideration. Generally following their model, we regressed on several independent

Table 4.10

Ratio of Constituent Service Hours to Total Hours Spent on City Business as a Function of Various Variables

Independent Variables	b	Standard Error
Form of election	22.83***	3.29
Ethnicity	21.5*	8.88
Number of years on city council	0.988	0.809
Previous political activity	−3.84	6.25
Constituent interests	10.20	5.94
Group focus	13.43***	3.01
Areal focus	4.67	3.29

Intercept = 39.66; R^2 (adj.) 0.09; $F = 8.81$; significance $p < 0.000$.
 *$p < 0.05$ level.
 ***$p < 0.000$ level.

variables the percentage of time spent on city business that was devoted to constituency service. In addition to ethnicity, form of election, number of years on the city council, council members' perceptions of the interests of their constituents, and previous political activity by the council member, we included the two representational foci from the factor analysis. If Clingermayer and Feiock are correct, then the representational focus should emerge as a significant variable. The data are presented in Table 4.10.

Three significant variables are found in the equation: form of election, ethnicity, and group representation focus. Those council members elected from districts tended to spend 22 percentage points more time doing constituency service for their constituents than did at-large council members, significantly more than Welch and Bledsoe found (1988, 73). Being Mexican American also greatly contributes to the percentage of time spent doing constituency service—21.5 percent. Interestingly, council members with a groups representational focus tend to report a significantly high percentage of constituency service. This may well be because these groups—labor, single interest, ideological, and business—are important to any council member's reelection constituency. The areal representational focus—which includes neighborhood and racial/ethnic group representation—does not emerge as a significant variable.

Table 4.11

Representational Factor Scores as a Function of Various Variables

	Factor 1	Factor 2
Independent Variables	Group	Areal
Form of election	0.04	0.54***
	(0.08)	(0.07)
Ethnicity	0.33**	0.78***
	(0.12)	(0.11)
Number of years on city council	0.00	0.03
	(0.01)	(0.03)
Previous political activity	0.10	0.10
	(0.08)	(0.07)
Constituent interests	−0.09	0.06
	(0.08)	(0.07)
Constituent service ratio	0.002***	0.0006
	(0.0005)	(0.0004)
Income	−0.19*	0.09
	(0.08)	(0.08)
Intercept	−0.09	−0.63**
	(0.18)	(0.12)
R^2 (adj.)	0.06	0.21
F	4.075	17.8
Significance	$p < 0.000$	$p < 0.000$

*$p < 0.05$ level.
**$p < 0.01$ level.
***$p < 0.000$ level.

To understand the nature of the representational focus more fully, we regressed the factor scores of the representational foci developed above on our main set of independent variables. The results are presented in Table 4.11.

The results indicate that the two representational foci are largely a function of different variables. Only one variable—ethnicity—is significant in both equations. The groups representational focus has ethnicity, income, and constituency service ratio as significant predictors of high factor scores on this representational focus. This is much as we would expect. Councilpersons who have a groups representational focus would be expected to pay attention to their constituency. Interestingly, Mexican American council members, as well as those councilpersons with lower incomes, tend to score high on this representational factor. It may be that this represents the tendency for these councilpersons to seek (and perhaps return) support from these groups. However, the amount of explanation provided by this equation is very modest. The equation for the second representational focus factor is somewhat more robust, explaining more than 21 percent of the variation in the factor scores. In this equation, form of election and ethnicity are both significant. Councilpersons elected by district elections and Mexican American councilpersons tend to score high on this representational focus. The regression coefficient for Mexican Americans is more than twice as large in this equation as it is for Mexican Americans in the first equation. In sum, this factor analysis explanation generally tends to support many of our expectations concerning the nature and impact of representation.

Ethnicity and Council Conflict

One of the unspoken assumptions of the urban reform movement was that the nonpartisan at-large electoral system would produce a city council that would speak in four-part harmony (see Browning, Marshall, and Tabb 1984; Heilig and Mundt 1984; and Welch and Bledsoe 1988). In this reformed world, all council members would have the same set of constituents—the city as a whole—and this should mute conflicting demands. The way in which the reformed council would make decisions would limit conflict. It is also important to note, however, that the process of decision making is also important. Heilig and Mundt (1984) have made clear the importance of access—of having a "voice at city hall." Thus, the way in which councils make decisions and the reaction among council members as well as the public are important aspects of policy in their own right. Councils may have little or no conflict, decisions may be made in unanimous or near-unanimous fashion, minorities may or may not be heard. All of these features are important aspects of council decision-making processes.

Heilig and Mundt (1984) have indicated that representatives with contrasting constituencies would exacerbate conflict in the deliberative processes of the council. They expected that at-large councils would have a higher degree of consensus than districted or mixed councils. However, their case study analysis did not strongly support this expectation. Browning, Marshall, and Tabb (1984, 141) have informed us that the mere presence of minority council members changed the decision-making processes of the city. Welch and Bledsoe (1988, 97) found partial support for their expectation that districted cities would experience greater conflict than at-large cities. They found that "election by district does slightly predispose a council to break into factions, independent of the size of the group" (1988, 99).

As with the Welch and Bledsoe study, our data are self-reported. That is, we asked our sample of council members a series of questions concerning their perception of decision making and conflict on the council. We were interested in the perceived level of conflict in different electoral structures and perceived direction of change. We also were interested in comparing the perceptions of Mexican American and Anglo councilpersons.

As expected, most of our respondents (73 percent) indicate that 75 percent or more of the decisions made by the city council are unanimous. However, a large number (26 percent) indicate the presence of voting blocs on the council. District councilpersons were more likely to indicate a low percentage of decisions as unanimous ($t = -2.62$; $p < 0.00$), to report an increase in council conflict ($t = -2.26$; $p < 0.05$), and to report that an increase in conflict had occurred since the change to a district form of elections ($t = -2.36$; $p < 0.05$). These findings generally are in accord with those of Welch and Bledsoe (1988, 94–99).

While the at-large councilpersons' reports of conflict were in line with our expectations, an interesting complication did arise. Some at-large councilpersons are elected in a true or "pure" at-large system. Other are elected to an at-large seat in a hybrid, or mixed, system, sharing a city council with persons elected from districts. It was our expectation that at-large council members elected in a mixed system would perceive higher levels of conflict than would those elected in a pure at-large system. Our data tend to support this expectation. At-large council members elected in mixed systems report the existence of voting blocs on the council more than do those at-large representatives from a pure system (53 percent versus 35 percent). Approximately the same percentage see most of the council decisions as unanimous (77 percent versus 73 percent). However, 30 percent of the mixed at-large representatives report an increase in council conflict compared with only 22 percent of "pure" at-large representatives.

In terms of ethnicity, Mexican American council members are more likely to report the existence of voting blocs on the city council (t = −2.71; $p < 0.00$) and less likely to report that a high percentage of decisions are made unanimously. Anglos are more likely to report that conflict on the council has increased following a change to a districted form of election (t = 3.84; $p < 0.000$).

Another aspect of the intracouncil dynamics is from the perspective of the city manager. Here we ask if changing from at-large to single-member districts results in a different type of council representative from the perspective of the city manager. In addition, we are interested in the interrelationships between members of the council and between the council and city manager. Heilig and Mundt (1984) suggest that city managers believe that district councilpersons are more likely to interfere with city operations. Browning, Marshall, and Tabb (1984, 204, 250) suggest a link between districts and weakened city managers. The role that the city manager plays, or would play, in a city council with expanded minority representation is critical. Traditionally, city managers play a facilitating and coordinating role in the development of policies (Morgan and Watson 1992, 438). It may be that city managers often find themselves playing similar roles in terms of ameliorating conflict within the council or building coalitions among council members. If Mexican American council members, who almost always will be in a minority status on the council, are to be effective, such coalitions must be built and maintained. Here we ask the question, What impact has the presence of district representatives had on the council itself? We conducted a series of unstructured, open-ended interviews with the city managers of our ten cities between 1986 and 1992. The interviews ranged from thirty-five minutes to ninety minutes. All but two of the city managers had served under both at-large and district systems. They ranged in age from the low thirties to the late fifties, and in experience from five years to over eighteen years. All were male; all but one were Anglo. Four of the ten were city manager when their city was districted. The respondents were guaranteed anonymity.

We asked the following questions. Had the change to districts made an overall difference in the representational link between the city council and the minority community? Had the change created more conflict on the council? More coalition building? What effect had the change had on the internal dynamics between the council and the manager? Which system, at-large or district, did the manager prefer?

The city managers were in almost total agreement that the change to districts had enhanced minority representation. Nine of the ten managers agreed that the change had resulted in a more representative council. Perhaps a bit surprising was the way many of the managers identified that change. "It's had no effect here," one said. "Oh, [Mexican Americans] get more representation, but *otherwise* [italics ours] it hasn't changed much." Another manager responded, "It's not very different from before. The [Mexican American council member] keeps a close watch on his district's needs, but *otherwise* [italics ours] there's been little change." That same manager noted that the Mexican American council member was the one member of the council most likely to perceive his district as a "constituency."

"There have been no substantial changes," a city manager from one of the larger cities stated. "Perhaps the minority community believes they are better represented, but I've noticed no other changes." He paused, then laughed and said, "Of course, that's an important change." Another manager continued this pattern when he observed that the weakness of redistricting is that the Mexican American neighborhoods seemed to focus primarily on their problems through their district representative, rather than on the problems of the community as a whole. One manager observed that Mexican American council members in his city were more likely than Anglos to focus on district needs. Again tacitly conceding a direct representational link, he said, "Anglos may be elected by both Anglos and Mexican Americans, but Mexican American candidates are elected primarily by Mexican American voters, so naturally the Mexican American members [of the council] will be more responsive." One city manager was unequivocal: "There's no question the district system provides better representation for minorities; the city council is more responsive to minority needs." Mexican American council members were described several times by several city managers as "advocates" and "showing the flag."

Many of the managers also noted substantive changes in the council procedures as a result of districting, changes that point to a more direct representational link with the Mexican American population. In two of the cities the traditional method of making board appointments was altered to provide more direct input from the council members. One city manager observed that the increased focus on minority districts had led to the formation of organized neighborhood groups that made political claims on the council. In one city the change to districts produced an increased emphasis on minority business enterprises. In one city with a hybrid system the tradition of designating the top vote getter among the council members as the mayor pro tem was discarded because district representatives would never receive as many votes overall as the at-large members. The pro tem position is now rotated.

What is clear from these responses is that in all but one of the ten cities, the city managers view the change to districts as having had a direct effect in linking the Mexican American community and the city council. If that perception is accurate, for the first time in many of the cities, Mexican Americans have a voice in city hall.

In response to other questions, all but one city manager agreed that the change to districts had created more conflict on the councils. That conflict was not viewed as necessarily negative, but rather as a natural consequence of what one manager termed "parochialism." Many of the city managers interviewed noted that after an initial period of conflict between ethnic council members and nonethnics, most council members began to work together. When issues came up that affected one of the district representative's constituents, the tendency was for other members of the council to defer to the district's representative, or to let the district representative act as "lead" for the council on that particular issue.

All but one of the city managers believed the change to districts had led to coalition construction between the council members, with most of the city managers noting that such "logrolling" was more evident during the budgeting process.

It appears, then, that one of the first impacts of the change to some form of district elections is the alteration of previously existing patterns of council dynamics.

Another way in which the shift to single-member districts has altered council dynamics is in the relationship of the city manager to the council. City managers with a district form of representation on their council may have to alter the way in which they approach their traditional role shaped in the at-large council–manager relationship. District representatives generally were more likely to have a more focused view of their relationship to the manager. Almost all the managers reported that the district representative requested more information from the manager's office. This is similar to the findings of Heilig and Mundt (1984).

One city manager said, "Now it's as if I have to deal with [several] little mayors." The way in which he deals with the council is to present his budget with breakouts for all districts in terms of such items as policing, drainage, and so on. He prefers this, however, to the previous at-large system, saying it enables him to engage in coalition building with the council members. Another city manager noted that when a district representative pushes for something in his or her district, the other council members are likely to ask for similar consideration. This manager cited the example of police patrols. One district representative, whose district had a higher crime rate than the rest of the city, obtained additional patrols for his area. Another council member then asked for additional patrols also, and, although his district had one of the lowest crime rates in the city, the district received additional patrols.

All but two of the ten city managers had served under both at-large and districted councils. When asked which they prefer, six preferred at-large systems; three, district systems; and one said it made no difference. Supporters of the at-large system believed it better enabled them to govern in the best interests of "the city as a whole" and avoided "ward or special interest politics." Those are, of course, some of the traditional arguments of the reform style of governance (Lineberry and Fowler 1967). The proponents of district elections believed it to be more "representative," "more open and visible." One manager suggested the district system allows "the city manager to avoid city council politics and forces the council members to negotiate with each other." Another noted that the district scheme diverted criticism that previously had been directed at the manager to the district representatives.

Overall, it is clear that, in the opinion of the city managers, the change to districts has had major impacts. Most important, perhaps, both those who prefer at-large systems and those who prefer districting agree that the change to districts results in a direct representational link between the Mexican American population and the city council.

Welch and Bledsoe (1988, 102) argue that the different levels of council conflict that they report are probably not based on policy differences, but on more "pork barrel" issues. While this might be so, we suggest that the differing representational/constituency foci of district-based and minority councilpersons lead to the expansion of levels of conflict. Also, we suggest that there might be unanimity or near unanimity on most issues, and intense conflict on only a few of major importance.

Table 4.12

Agreement with Unfettered Development Policy as a Function of Various Variables

Independent Variables	b	Standard Error
Form of election	−0.14	0.11
Ethnicity	−0.41**	0.14
Number of years on city council	−0.01	0.01
Previous political activity	0.17	0.09
Constituent interests	0.13	0.10
Group focus	−0.03	0.05
Areal focus	−0.16**	0.05
Constituent service ratio	0.001	0.0006

Intercept = 2.85; R^2 (adj.) = 0.05; F 4.54; significance $p < 0.000$.
**$p < 0.01$ level.

Policy Congruence

A major, indeed, fundamental role of urban policy makers is to focus on the economic development of the community, even though it is difficult for many cities effectively to compete (Schneider 1989). Given the overwhelming importance of this issue, it makes a good test of policy congruence among council members. If, as Welch and Bledsoe (1988) suggest, conflict is not policy based, then there should be relatively high levels of agreement on this issue.

We examined council members' views on economic policy and their relationship to the representational foci noted above, as well as other explanatory variables. We asked council members to agree or disagree with this statement: "Generally, I approve of unlimited development in the city; if business wants to invest in new housing or new businesses, the city should go along."[10] We regressed agreement with this question on the representational foci derived from the factor analysis, method of election, ethnicity of council member, number of years the council member had served on the city council, the previous political activity of the council member, the council member's view of his or her constituent interests, and the amount of time the council member spent in constituency service as a ratio of all time spent on city business. The results are presented in Table 4.12.

Two significant variables contribute to disagreement with unfettered development policy: ethnicity and areal focus. Mexican American council members and those council members with an areal representational focus tend to disagree with the statement. Although the R^2 is very modest, the two variables that are significant and the direction of the regression coefficients support our assumptions. Our results suggest that there is a disposition on the part of minority council members and those with an areal representational focus not to support unfettered development policy. It may be that, as Clingermayer and Feiock (1993) note, casework in relation to municipal economic development policy is not a good test, that it might be fundamentally different from other policy areas. It also may well be that ethnic council members and council members with the areal representational focus simply do not support unfettered development. Much of the "urban renewal" type of urban development schemes resulted in massive dislocation of ethnic enclaves and minority neighborhoods, so it may not be surprising that these council members are less enthusiastic about economic development in the city. Also, the conception may well be that the benefits of the economic development policy might not "trickle down" to their constituents. This issue area, however, might also suggest policy disagreement as one very real source of conflict among council members.

Summary and Conclusions

One of the major assumptions of the urban reform movement of the late nineteenth and early twentieth centuries was that such structural reforms as nonpartisanship and at-large elections would result in the election of a different type of city council member—one with a concern for the city as a whole, and not indebted to political machines. In large part this did happen. However, the late twentieth century re-reforms, stimulated in part by the Voting Rights Act, have altered the impact of the early reformers. With the adoption of district elections, more council members are selected who represent a different socioeconomic group, especially in terms of ethnicity. The change to district election structures in Texas has resulted in more Mexican Americans being elected to city councils. Also, council members with a decidedly neighborhood orientation have been elected.

Our data show that there are significant differences between council members elected by district and those elected at-large. The data also show that there are significant differences between Mexican American council members and Anglo council members. District council members report that they were persuaded to seek local elective office by, and received support from, neighborhood groups. Once they are in office, it is clear that the ethnic and district council members adopt a different style of work and orientation. They tend to spend more time than their at-large counterparts in general on city business, and more time particularly performing constituent services. While it might not be accurate to term the council members "errand boys," it is clear that these members have a constituency service orientation quite distinct from that of the at-large council members and the Anglo council members. This representational and constituency focus distinction may help explain the existence of voting blocs, levels of conflict, and the reported increase in conflict among council members.

While council members in general are well-educated, moderate conservative males, Mexican American council members tend to be somewhat younger, less well educated, and more conservative than their Anglo counterparts. They also are more likely than Anglos to view the city council as a stepping-stone to higher political office. We believe the latter point is particularly important. It is likely that city council elections will be the first step on the path to higher political office for Mexican American public officials; these campaigns will provide valuable experience for later campaigns, experience that previously had been denied to this particular group. The most prominent example, but certainly not the only example, of this development is Henry Cisneros, whose movement to national recognition began with his election to the newly districted San Antonio city council.

Changing from at-large to district systems is viewed by the courts as a remedy for past discrimination against Mexican Americans. Conventional wisdom holds that district elections will enhance the chances of Mexican American candidates. An equally important goal, one that goes beyond the symbolic gains of electoral victories and extends beyond passive representation, is to translate electoral victories into substantive policy changes for the Mexican American community.

Notes

1. The work by Meier and Stewart (1991) provides an excellent overview of the nature of representation. The following section draws heavily upon the work of Meier and Stewart, especially chapter 4.

2. Professor Susan Welch was kind enough to make her survey instrument available to us and to allow us to use major portions of it for this study. Much of this chapter is an attempt to replicate the Welch and Bledsoe (1988) study, focusing on one state and including smaller cities in the analysis. We are, of course, heavily indebted to Professors Welch and Bledsoe for their work.

3. We used the WEIGHT command in SPSS. As is generally known, tests of statistical significance are based on the weighted or reweighted sample size. Thus, one runs a considerable risk when using weighting procedures (SPSS, Inc. 1988). To avoid inflating the statistical significance levels, one should use a weight factor that, when summed, is the same as the unweighted number of cases (SPSS, Inc. 1988, 189). Thus, these analyses are based on the reweighted number of cases equal to that of the original survey.

4. Our questionnaire asked council members the form of electoral structure under which they were elected: "What type of election system is used in your community? If mixed, from which form are you elected?" Thus, we were able to isolate all council members elected from districts and those elected from at-large systems. Our conceptualization is on the individual level.

5. The form of our question was virtually identical to that of question one in the Welch and Bledsoe instrument: "We would like to know why you initially decided to seek election to the city/town council. Please rate the importance of each of the following factors in influencing your decision to run for a council seat. Circle best response."

6. Our use of this one question does not constitute a full test of Schlesinger's (1966) theory of ambition in the sense that we did not test for discrete or static ambitions and focused on ambition only in the sense of identifying reasons for seeking local office. It may well be that this limited exploration does not fully capture the manifold-ambition concept. Some local legislators might become ambitious after leaving office.

7. The question was, "How important were each of the following in your last campaign in terms of giving money, helping in your campaign in some way, or providing other kinds of support?" The six groups identified were: your political party, organized labor, business groups or leaders, neighborhood organizations, organized racial or ethnic groups, and groups organized over a single issue.

8. The question was identical to the Welch and Bledsoe (1988) formulation: "Council members represent many different constituencies. In your own view, how important is your representation of each of the following constituencies?" Council members were asked to rate each on a three-point scale.

9. These questions were: "Approximately how many hours per week do you devote to your job as a member of the city council?" and "Of the total number of hours per week, how many do you spend doing services for people?" Both questions were drawn from the Welch and Bledsoe (1988) survey.

10. As before, this statement was taken from the Welch and Bledsoe (1988) study.

5

Electoral Structure and School Board Member Attitudes

Americans have long disassociated school districts from other units of government. Campbell et al. (1985, 79) note that school districts have enjoyed this distinction because the public refuses to associate anything as fundamental as education with the "muck and mire" of practical politics. In essence, many Americans, aided and abetted by the educational establishment, treat school district policies and educational policies in a decidedly nonpolitical way. That this mindset has tremendous impact on educational policies and practices is easily seen. Schools generally have been exempted from the consideration of political and policy concern accorded other services provided to consumers.

It is clear that education and access to educational resources are among the most important of all urban services. Education is probably the most "reformed" of all urban political institutions, although it has not traditionally been considered an "urban service" (Meier, Stewart, and England 1991). Public education in this country historically has been under local control. The school systems not only educate students, they are important forms of political socialization, and often serve as the most significant employer in an area. State and local governments spend almost one-half of their revenue on education, so education is important both in terms of policy outputs and as a significant policy resource. Chubb and Moe describe the historical development of American education:

> Schooling was a local affair. Basic issues of organization and control—
> issues that today would be classified as budgeting, curriculum, person-
> nel, purchasing, accountability and the like . . . tended to be handled by

the people closest to each school: parents, interested citizens, and their elected representatives. In urban areas, party organizations sometimes had a hand in orchestrating all this, and they saw to it that their interests in patronage and the letting of contracts were furthered. But even in these settings, authority was highly decentralized and afforded the lower classes and ethnic and religious minorities control over their own schools. (1990, 3)

Levin (1970) argues that this tradition of local control remained reasonably ensured as long as large segments of the community maintained a strong interest in the schools. As he put it, "Since schools directly affect the lives of many families and the local governing board would be the first major elective effort of the community, the residents would not be indifferent to election outcomes or community school practices" (1970, 289).

The reform movement generally associated with the progressive era has been credited with changing much of this system and turning the educational system into a highly bureaucratized and professionalized institution (Tyack 1974). Power was transferred from the local citizens to a professional bureaucracy that was assumed to know what educational services to provide and how to provide them efficiently. Central to this developing professionalism was the creation of locally elected school boards, generally running at-large under nonpartisan labels and making policy decisions under the supervision of both state law and the state educational bureaucracy. Chubb and Moe argue that the losers in this shift to professionalism included "the lower classes, ethnic and religious minorities, and citizens of rural communities. Their traditional control over local schools was now largely transferred to the new system's political and administrative authorities" (1990, 4). As Just puts it, "By the 1890s, another educational reform movement was beginning. . . . reforms largely in place by the 1920s provided stability to urban school governance and perpetuated the 'apolitical' character of public school management through the mid-twentieth century" (1980, 421–22).

Iannaccone and Lutz (1970) identify several distinctive features of contemporary local school district governance that help to strengthen the reforms. They argue that the fiscal independence of the local school district, the fact that school districts generally are not coterminous with other local governments, and the practice of holding separate elections combine to make the reformed system independent of other governments (Iannaccone and Lutz 1970, 10–12). This independence marks one of the most significant of all the features of American school districts. Not only are school districts independent legally, but most Americans think of them as nongovernmental in nature. In effect, the reform movement took education and educational policy making out of the American policy-making system.

Significant societal changes also influenced the development of the local educational system. Among the most important of these was the historic desegregation of American public schools following *Brown* v. *Board of Education* in 1954. The movement to desegregate the public schools, for the most part, was led by forces outside the professional educational bureaucracy. This may, in part, reflect the absence of minority members on the at-large school boards, as the at-large procedures usually shut out minorities. At-large elections generally also are credited with depressing voting turnout. Zeigler and his colleagues say, "At-large elections depress the levels of competition. . . . at-large elections appear to scare potential candidates away from competing for office" (1974, 59).

Meier, Stewart, and England (1991) conducted one major study that examines access to educational resources as an urban service. They argue that educational policy is the urban service most likely to be controlled by bureaucratic decisions. Indeed, substantial research has found that the policy-making body of the educational system (the local school board) has largely become subservient to the professional educators (Zeigler, Jennings, and Peak 1974). Zeigler and his colleagues say:

> Such behavior and attitudes add up to a board with primary identification with the superintendent, a negation of the role normally associated with representatives of the community. . . . the job of a board member becomes one of supporting the administration's program. (1974, 166–67)

Lutz concurs with this point of view when he notes, "The vast majority [of school board members] respect—even revere—the superintendent as the professional expert, looking to the superintendent, almost exclusively, for recommendations and information and for the implementation of policies they exact upon his or her recommendation" (1980, 459).

The reform movement's goal of shifting from ward-based elections to at-large elections was achieved. Zeigler, Kehoe, and Reisman report that almost 73 percent of school districts have pure at-large elections, and that of the school districts in the forty-nine largest cities, more than 80 percent elect their board members by at-large systems (1985, 11).

We have noted earlier that schools are among the most reformed of American political institutions and that the election of minority school board members is an integral part of the process of improving educational access for minority children. The preceding chapter provided a macro-level focus on Texas electoral districts. Here, we provide a micro-level focus on these concerns, examining the attitudes of school board members toward selected issues and, in concert with chapter 4, providing a comparison of elected local officials in two institutional settings: cities and school boards.

We are interested in such issues as the demographics of school board members, the impact of electoral structure on the recruitment of school board members, the impact of electoral structure on the relationships within the school board, the mode of representation practiced by school board members, and the distinctive policy orientations held by these public officials.

As we suggested in the previous chapter, being concerned about the priorities of the people they represent can be thought of as part of the representative bureaucracy component wherein elected officials share the same background, attitudes, and priorities of those whom they represent (Meier and Stewart 1991; Mosher 1968). That is, race and ethnicity act as socializing agents to strengthen the linkage between passive and active representation for minority legislators. Ethnicity can be salient in regard to how legislators and/or bureaucrats define their representational role. We believe this is especially true for those policy makers who represent minority districts or communities. It may well be especially important for elected school board members. Lyke (1968, 156–57) argues that education politics lack sufficient representation, owing in part to a lack of diversity among the political representatives who fashion educational policy. He argues that, as a general rule, school board members all tend to be elected by the same constituency.

Methodology

These data are from a survey of school board members during the spring of 1993. We surveyed all school boards in Texas that had changed from at-large elections to some form of districting during the

1980s. We also surveyed a control sample of school districts that had not changed their electoral structures, matching on size, ethnicity of student body, and location in state. A second mailing of the survey targeted those members who had not responded to the first wave. One hundred and fifty school boards made up the total sample, seventy-five from each group. A total of 674 usable responses were obtained, for a response rate of 64.2 percent. The survey instrument was modeled after Welch and Bledsoe (1988), thus allowing comparability with the city council data. We compared the means of the two waves of our sample on a number of socioeconomic dimensions, including age, ethnicity, education, and income, and found no significant differences between the first and second wave. Unlike Welch and Bledsoe, we found that responses to the second wave were as complete as the first wave in terms of the open-ended items. Response rates did differ somewhat according to the different ethnic or racial group. Mexican American school board members had a response rate of 54.7 percent, African American school board members had a rate of 51.8 percent, and Anglo school board members responded at the highest rate—66.5 percent.

In addition to descriptive summaries, we use measures of association including t-tests and correlations in addition to multivariate analyses of OLS regression and logistic regression.

Who Are the School Board Members?

Table 5.1 offers a general description of our respondent pool. School board members tend to be well educated, with almost three-fourths having either a college or postgraduate degree. They tend to hold white-collar jobs with comfortable incomes (over one-half make more than $65,000 per year). They are mostly Anglo males with an average age of forty-nine years, and they have lived in their community more than half of their lives. The characteristics of our Texas school board sample fit well with other studies of school board membership. Most studies find that school board members are very well educated, are in high-status professions, and are overwhelmingly from the dominant Anglo culture (Campbell et al. 1985, 181). The bias of most school boards is well documented. Very few minorities make it.

Board members have served an average of 4.9 years on the school board. They are overwhelmingly conservative to moderate in political

Table 5.1

Descriptive Information on School Board Members

Gender:	
Male	73%
Female	27
Income:	
35,000	11%
$35,000–64,999	35
$65,000+	54
Occupation:	
Prof./mgr.	68%
Other	32
Education:	
High school	7%
Some college	19
College grad.	33
Prof./grad.	41
Ethnicity:	
Mexican American	14%
Anglo	86
Ideology:	
Conservative	60%
Moderate	25
Liberal	15
Average age	49
Years in community	27
Average size of board	7
Average years on board	4.9

ideology, with only 15 percent identifying themselves as liberal; three-fifths of our respondents said they were conservative.

Table 5.2 distinguishes respondents on the basis of ethnicity. There is little difference in terms of gender or age. However, on several other measures there are statistically significant differences between Anglo and Mexican American school board members. The average Mexican American school board member is less well educated, with less than half possessing a college degree. Mexican American board members are less likely than Anglo board members to hold white-collar jobs and to be found in the upper income bracket. In striking contrast, Mexican

Table 5.2

Differences between Anglo and Mexican American School Board Members

	Anglo	Mexican American
Gender:		
Male	72%	78%
Female	28	22
Income***		
<$35,000	9%	20%
$35,000–64,999	32	52
$65,000+	59	28
Occupation**		
Prof./mgr.	70%	54%
Other	30	46
Education***		
High school	4%	20%
Some college	17	30
College grad.	34	29
Prof./grad.	45	20
Ideology***		
Conservative	66%	36%
Moderate	22	40
Liberal	12	24
Average age	40	42
Years in community***	25.8	33.4
Average size of board	7	7
Average years on board***	5	4.5

**Mean of Anglo significantly different from Mexican American at 0.01 level.
***Mean of Anglo significantly different from Mexican American at 0.000 level.

American board members are much more likely to identify themselves as moderate to liberal, while most Anglos view themselves as moderate to conservative. Mexican American board members are likely to have resided longer in the community than their Anglo counterparts, but tend to have served less time on the school boards. We also asked the school board members to indicate their support for a variety of policy questions that might face local school boards. These ranged from raising taxes or cutting services, to allow unfettered development within the school district, distributing resources within the district by need, and requiring more drug education and more family planning in the schools. On only two issues were the differences between Mexican American and Anglos statistically significant. Anglos slightly preferred more drug education in schools (t = −2.23, significance = 0.027), while Mexican Americans slightly preferred more family planning in schools (t = −1.96, significance = 0.052). On all our other policy issues there were no significant differences between Anglos and Mexican Americans.

The differences noted here paint a picture of differences, based on ethnicity, among the school board members. We have noted earlier the salient role that ethnicity can play in representational role definition. Given that, and these demographic differences, we expect that Anglos and Mexican Americans will define their representational roles on the school boards differently.

Tenure, Gender, and Ideology

We explore here the relationship between electoral structure and the ethnicity and socioeconomic characteristics of school board members.[1]

When we distinguish respondents on the basis of electoral structure, we find some statistically significant differences. Table 5.3 shows that at-large representatives are more likely than district representatives to enjoy high incomes. Looked at from another angle, this would seem to indicate that district elections offer opportunities to less-well-financed candidates that at-large elections do not. This difference also correlates with other socioeconomic variables. That is, district board members are less likely than at-large members to hold white-collar jobs and are less likely also to possess college or professional and graduate degrees. These data fit well with Welch and Bledsoe's findings concerning the effect of district elections with respect to city councils (1988, 50). We see also that Anglos are more likely than Mexican Americans to be elected from at-large seats, and Mexican Americans are more likely to be elected from districts. In addition, we find that there is a statistically significant relationship concerning the years spent on the school board (district members have, on the average, been on the board for fewer years) and between the years spent residing in the community (district representatives are likely to have lived in the community longer than at-large representatives).

Other than these factors, most differences reported are relatively

Table 5.3

Differences between School Board Members Elected At-Large and by District (in %)

	At-Large	District
Gender:		
Male	73	73
Female	27	27
Income:		
<$35,000	7	20
$35,000–64,999	34	52
$65,000+	59	28***
Occupation:		
Prof./mgr.	71	54
Other	29	46***
Education:		
High school	4	11
Some college	15	26
College grad.	33	32
Prof./grad.	48	31***
Ethnicity:		
Mexican American	12	19
Anglo	88	81**
Ideology:		
Conservative	61	58
Moderate	24	26
Liberal	15	16
Average age	48	48
Years in community	25.4	30.2***
Average size of board	7	7
Average years on board	5.1	4.5*

*Mean of district significantly different from at-large at 0.05 level.
**Mean of district significantly different from at-large at 0.01 level.
***Mean of district significantly different from at-large at 0.000 level.

minor and not statistically significant. District board members were not significantly different ideologically from at-large board members. Both tend to be conservative to moderate. Some of the research literature suggests that women are more likely to be disadvantaged by district elections (Welch and Karnig 1979). Our data do not support this. There is no significant difference in gender representation between the two types of electoral systems. In each system, approximately one-fourth of the school board members are female. It is interesting to note that there is quite substantially greater representation of females on school boards than on city councils (27 percent versus 18 percent). Cassel (1985) argues that nonpartisan elections produce higher-status council members than do partisan elections. If we carry this proposition further, the greater proportion of women on school boards would seem to reflect the higher-status/nonpolitical nature of school boards. It would seem that school boards are "safe" political venues for female office holders.

Motivation for Seeking Office

We asked the school board members why they initially decided to seek election to the board.[2] We also asked them to rate each of seven items on a scale of importance. The potential reasons included responses that indicate strong issue concern, representational foci on either the district as a whole or the representative's own neighborhood, an indication of progressive political ambition, recruitment by a political party, and personal reasons such as enjoying politics and increasing business contacts. Table 5.4 reports those findings. Only two statistically significant differences between district members and at-large members show up. District board members are more likely than at-large members to identify service to their neighborhood as a reason for seeking public office (89 percent versus 70 percent). As in the previous chapter, we would expect that board members who report this motivation for seeking office would tend to have an areal representational focus (see Clingermayer and Feiock 1993; Welch and Bledsoe 1988). We also found a statistically significant relationship with regard to the impact of single-issue politics. District board members are more likely than at-large members to run for office in response to a concern over a specific issue (72 percent versus 62 percent). The most common special concern was a generalized "quality of education" issue.

In the main, then, both district and at-large school board members share generally similar reasons for running for office. More than half of each group indicated that enjoyment of politics contributed to their decision to seek office. Neither group reported significant political ambitions, with less than one in ten seeking election to the school board as a stepping-stone to higher office. As noted in chapter 4, the

Table 5.4

Differences between School Board Members Elected At-Large and by District on Reasons for Seeking Local Office (in %)

	Importance	At-Large	District
Because I was persuaded by a political party organization.	No	90	91
	Yes	10	9
To serve my neighborhood.	No	30	11
	Yes	70	89***
As a stepping-stone to other political office.	No	94	95
	Yes	6	5
To serve the district as a whole.	No	1	0
	Yes	99	100
To increase business contacts.	No	93	94
	Yes	7	6
Because I enjoy politics.	No	38	30
	Yes	62	70
Because of a strong concern I had about some specific issue.	No	38	28
	Yes	62	72*

*Mean of district significantly different from at-large at 0.05 level.
***Mean of district significantly different from at-large at 0.000 level.

lack of political ambition among local policy makers comports with previous research that suggests that those at higher levels of office—state rather than local—are more likely to be politically ambitious (Burt-Way and Kelly 1991, 15).

Ethnicity, Motivations, and Political Support

We also examined the motivations for seeking office by ethnicity. We asked, in essence, whether Mexican American school board members were motivated to seek office for reasons different from Anglo board members. Table 5.5 reports the data concerning motivation.

Mexican Americans and Anglos share similar motivations for seeking election to their school board; even in the three areas where there are statistically significant differences, the direction of motivation is

Table 5.5

Differences between Anglo and Mexican American School Board Members on Reasons for Seeking Local Office (in %)

	Importance	Anglo	Mexican American
Because I was persuaded by a political party organization.	No	91	83
	Yes	9	17
To serve my neighborhood.	No	25	9
	Yes	75	91***
As a stepping stone to other political office.	No	95	94
	Yes	5	6
To serve the district as a whole.	No	6	0
	Yes	92	100
To increase business contacts.	No	94	92**
	Yes	6	8
Because I enjoy politics.	No	34	34
	Yes	66	66
Because of a strong concern I had about some specific issue.	No	38	12***
	Yes	62	88

**Mean of Mexican Americans significantly different from Anglos at 0.01 level.
***Mean of Mexican Americans significantly different from Anglos at 0.001 level.

the same for both ethnic groups. The statistically significant differences occur in terms of running for office in order to serve the candidate's neighborhood, in order to increase business contacts, and because of a strong concern about a specific issue. Mexican Americans were more likely to seek office in order to serve their neighborhoods (91 percent versus 75 percent). Mexican Americans were slightly less likely than Anglos to run in order to increase business contacts (92 percent versus 94 percent). Finally, Mexican Americans were more likely than Anglos to be motivated to run for office out of concern for a specific issue (88 percent versus 62 percent).

No other motivation for seeking office is significant, and there is little difference based on ethnicity with respect to the remaining motivating factors. Neither ethnic group views running for the school board as preparation for seeking higher office, nor is either ethnic group motivated to run as a result of political party contact. Both ethnic groups express identical positive attitudes toward politics (66 percent) as an influence on their decision to seek office.

We expanded our analyses of the reasons for seeking local elective office by estimating a logistic regression equation on all six of the reasons given, with form of election, ethnicity, size of city, the ideology of the council member, previous political activity of the council member, and council member's view of constituent interests as independent. This logistic regression allows us to assess the relative significance of each of these independent variables, taken as a whole. The results of the analyses are reported in Table 5.6.

The table reports four regressions. These were the only significant equations. The four significant equations do classify an adequate percentage of cases and have significant model chi-squares. We did not find some expected relationships: most important, ethnicity is not significant in any equation. Form of election, ideology, and board members' perceptions of their constituents' interests are significant in one equation. Only the absence of previous political activity is significant in more than one equation. Community size does not affect school board members' reasons for seeking office. The size of the city is not significant in any equation.

As we anticipated, district school board members report serving the neighborhood as an important reason for seeking office. Those persons without prior political experience report being influenced to run for office by their response to particular issues and by their perception that politics is a fulfilling endeavor.

Respondents who identify themselves as more liberal indicated that they were likely to be motivated to run for office in response to particular issues. Finally, respondents who rated constituent interests as a high priority believed that serving one's neighborhood was an important motivating factor in the decision to seek office.

There appears, then, to be no single motivation for seeking office that characterizes school board candidates; rather, there are a variety of motivations distinguished by the school district's election structure, the candidate's political ideology, the candidate's perception of constituents' interests, and the candidate's previous political experience, or lack thereof.

It is clear that school board members overwhelmingly reject progressive political ambition as a motivation for seeking local office. Burt-Way and Kelly (1991, 14) find that the dominant political aspira-

Table 5.6

Logistic Regression of Importance of Reasons for Seeking Local Office: School Boards

Independent Variables	Political Party	Serve Neighbor-hood	Special Issues	Enjoy Politics
City size	0.41	−0.09	0.08	0.26
	(0.31)	(0.21)	(0.19)	(0.19)
Form of election	−0.09	1.16***	0.26	−0.34
	(0.32)	(0.25)	(0.19)	(0.19)
Ethnicity	−0.09	0.17	0.19	0.10
	(0.23)	(0.17)	(0.16)	(0.13)
Previous political activity	−0.17	0.10	−0.90***	−1.14***
	(0.32)	(0.22)	(0.21)	(0.19)
Ideology	0.57	−0.24	0.40*	0.10
	(0.30)	(0.21)	(0.19)	(0.19)
Constituents' interests	−1.25	−0.68*	0.24	−0.02
	(0.31)	(0.29)	(0.22)	(0.23)
Intercept		1.41	0.80	0.12
% correctly classified	91	76	65	68
Model chi-square	19.6	34.7	31.0	43.8
DF	6	6	6	6
Significance	$p < 0.000$	$p < 0.000$	$p < 0.000$	$p < 0.000$

Standard errors in parentheses.
*$p < 0.05$ level.
***$p < 0.01$ level.

tion of local office holders is to continue to serve in their present position. At the same time, particular issues and the high rating of constituent interests do seem to be motivating forces. In short, our "typical" school board member is a high-status individual motivated not so much by personal gain or interest as by a selfless desire to serve. That this appears to be virtually the model of school board membership envisioned by the reform movement is testimony to its staying power.

School boards and school districts remain among the most reformed of American political institutions.

Representational Styles

We have identified two representational foci: representation where the focus is on one's election district rather than on the city or school district as a whole and representation where the focus is on the city or school district as a whole rather than on one's electoral district. We expect, of course, that representatives elected by district would tend to focus on their electoral district needs, while at-large representatives would tend to focus on the needs of the school district as a whole.

Welch and Bledsoe discussed these expected differences between at-large and district elected representatives in terms of city council elections; we speculate that the same notions would apply to school district representatives. They said:

> Those elected at-large will be more likely than those elected by district to believe that they "represent the city as a whole"; those elected by district will be more likely to see themselves representing neighborhood or ethnic constituencies. We might expect at-large representatives to be more likely to feel they represent business constituencies, than those elected by district labor constituencies. (1988, 59)

We asked school board members to assess the relative importance they attach to representing those different constituencies.[3] Table 5.7 reports the responses based on ethnicity and based on whether the respondent is elected at-large or from a district.

We look first at the responses based on ethnicity. We find a statistically significant difference between Mexican American school board members and Anglo school board members on every representational measure; all but one difference are in the expected direction. It is no surprise that Mexican American board members were more likely than Anglo board members to say that representation of organized labor, single-issue groups, neighborhood organizations, and racial or ethnic groups is important; these responses fit with the perception that Mexican Americans are more likely to reflect electoral district rather than district-wide concerns. Unexpectedly, we see also that Mexican Americans are more likely than Anglo board members to identify the representation of business groups as important.

Table 5.7

Differences between Anglo and Mexican American School Board Members and between At-Large and District Elections on Representational Foci (in %)

	Importance	Anglo	Mexican American	District	At-Large
Organized labor	No	90	72	87	86
	Yes	10	28***	13	14
Business groups	No	79	63	74	77
	Yes	21	37**	26	23
Neighborhood organizations	No	63	26	36	66
	Yes	37	74***	64	34###
Racial or ethnic groups	No	80	28	38	74
	Yes	20	72***	62	26##
Single-issue group	No	81	57	72	80
	Yes	19	43***	28	20#

**Mean of Mexican Americans significantly different from Anglos at 0.01 level.
***Mean of Mexican Americans significantly different from Anglos at 0.000 level.
#Mean of district council members significantly different from at-large council members at 0.05 level.
##Mean of district council members significantly different from at-large council members at 0.01 level.
###Mean of district council members significantly different from at-large council members at 0.000 level.

While we find fewer statistically significant differences between board members elected by district and those elected at-large, the differences are all in the expected directions. School board members elected at-large are less likely than district board members to focus on representing neighborhood organizations, racial or ethnic groups, or single-issue groups.

To expand our analyses of these patterns of representational foci, we performed a correlational analysis and a factor analysis on these data. The findings are reported in Table 5.8.

We expected the largest correlation to be between neighborhood and race; this turns out to be the case (0.44). The largest negative relationship is that of labor and city as a whole (−0.06). As was the case with

Table 5.8

Various Representational Foci

(A) Intercorrelations

Subject	Neighbor-hood	City	Ideology	Business	Single Interest	Race	Labor
Neighborhood	0.04	0.21	0.24	0.20	0.44	0.18	
City		−0.02	0.00	0.00	−0.02	−0.06	
Ideology			0.16	0.33	0.29	0.21	
Business				0.22	0.22	0.40	
Single interest					0.29	0.31	
Race						0.28	
Labor							

(B) Factor Analysis

Foci	Factor I Group Focus	Factor II Bus./Labor Focus	Factor III Areal Focus
Neighborhood	0.80		
Racial/ethnic group	0.77		
Business		0.78	
Labor		0.77	
City as a whole			0.91
Eigenvalue	2.00	1.15	1.00
Percentage of variation explained	28.7	16.5	14.3

our city council analyses, we found a positive relationship between business and neighborhood foci (0.24) where a negative one had been expected.

The factor analysis is presented in Table 5.8(B). Three factors emerged: a groups focus factor, a business/labor focus factor, and an areal focus factor. These three factors indicate three clusters of representational foci. The groups focus factor has two foci, both of which load positively; it explains almost 29 percent of the variation. The business/labor factor also has two positive loading foci. This factor explains 16.5 percent of the variation. The final factor, areal focus, has one positive focus: the city as a whole. This factor explains 14.3 percent of the variation.

In an attempt to explain the nature of these representational foci

Table 5.9

Regression of Factor 1 Scores on Various Independent Variables

Independent Variables	b	Standard Error
Form of election	0.232***	0.07
Ethnicity	0.220**	0.06
Ideology	0.151*	0.07
Years on board	0.009	0.01
Mexican American–Anglo TAAS ratio	0.0005	0.003
Total revenue per student	0.0009*	0.0004
Percentage Mexican American teachers	0.005**	0.001
Intercept	−0.76**	0.29

R^2 (adj.) = 0.09; F = 9.3; significance < 0.000.
　*$p < 0.05$.
　**$p < 0.01$.
　***$p < 0.000$.

more fully, we regressed each of the factor scores on a set of independent variables that included form of election, ethnicity, ideology, and number of years served on the board, as well as some information concerning the school district (see Table 5.9). The school district variables included a ratio of percentage of Mexican Americans to Anglos passing the Texas Assessment of Academic Skills test (TAAS—an exit test), the total revenue per pupil in the school district, and the percentage of Mexican American teachers. The exit test ratio was designed as a comparison of how well Mexican American students were doing in the district. The total revenue variable was included to control for disparities in wealth between districts. The Mexican American teacher variable was included because of the importance of teachers both as role models and as instructional leaders to minority students (see Meier and Stewart 1991). Only factor 1, the groups factor, produced a significant equation. Although the equation is not as robust as we might want, it is clear that several of our independent variables are significant. School board members who are elected from districted structures and Mexican American school board members have high positive coefficients. Interestingly, ideology (being more liberal) also has a fairly high positive coefficient. Total revenue per student and percentage of Mexican American teachers also significantly affect the factor score.

Representation and Board Member Behavior

Based in part on our findings in city councils as well as the Heilig and Mundt study (1984), we expect that different clusters of representational foci will produce different behavior on the part of the school board members. Again, we cite Clingermayer and Feiock; although they speak to the behavior of city council members, there is little reason to doubt the applicability to school board members: "Differences in the interests that are represented should also entail differences in the issues with which city legislators choose to involve themselves and the stances that they take toward those issues" (1993, 201).

One way to examine these differences is to look at perceived levels of conflict among school board members. Newman and Rice (1992) found a relationship between perceived levels of conflict on school boards and influence on the decision-making process. Specifically, they found that those school boards that perceived themselves as being rarely unanimous and often in opposing blocs also perceived the greatest amount of community involvement in school affairs (Newman and Brown 1992, 4). Interestingly, the group with high perceived conflict also found the superintendent as least influential. Our findings indicate that there is conflict on many school boards. A majority of our respondents indicated that there were no voting blocs on the school board (59 percent versus 41 percent). More than 90 percent of the respondents indicate that more than 75 percent of the decisions of the school board are unanimous. However, a rather substantial 27 percent indicate that conflict has increased during their service on the board. There are some distinctions among school board members based on electoral structure and ethnicity, although not as much as on the city councils. School board members elected from districts are more likely to indicate that voting blocs exist (t = -2.77; $p < 0.01$). Mexican American school board members are more likely than Anglos to believe that voting blocs exist (t = -2.49; $p < 0.05$).

Another way to look at differences is to examine what Eulau and Karps term "service responsiveness" (1978, 62). As we have noted earlier, there is considerable literature exploring this notion, including Brown, Fuchs, and Hoadley (1979), Cain, Ferejohn, and Fiorina (1979), and McAdams (1980). Response to constituent needs is, of course, a vital link between any elected official and his or her constituency; no elected official interested in being reelected ignores this link. School board members are unlikely to have very much staff support to aid in responding to constituent demands; consequently, they must, in the main, be responsible for these responses themselves.

We asked respondents to indicate how many hours per week they spent on school board business and how much of that time was spent on constituency service activities.[4] We examined these responses in terms of ethnicity and in terms of the form of election (not reported in tabular form). We did find statistically significant differences between Mexican American school board members and Anglo school board members. Mexican American board members tend to spend more hours than Anglos on school board business (10.7 versus 8.0) and also tend to work more hours on constituency services (6.2 versus 4.0).

In sum, we find a more service-oriented perspective on the part of school board members. As discussed above, we expected to find that ethnicity significantly affects the behavior of elected officials. The tendency of Mexican Americans to devote more time to school board business and more hours to constituency service would seem to indicate that our expectations are realized. Ethnicity does not play a significant role in distinguishing motivations for seeking local school board membership. However, once on the board, Mexican Americans and Anglos do demonstrate significantly different behavior. Much of the school board literature (see Tucker and Zeigler 1977; Campbell et al. 1985) indicates that board members tend to be relatively passive or quiescent. Mexican American school board members differ somewhat from this pattern. When we control for form of election, the difference is more extreme. Mexican American school board members elected by district spend a significantly larger amount of time on school board matters and on constituency service than do Anglos or other Mexican Americans elected at-large. Without controlling for form of ethnicity, we found no statistically significant differences between school board members elected at-large and those elected by districts.

We also examined the school board members' views on a range of policy questions, but found only a few differences based on ethnicity or form of election structure. Apparently, for school boards, what conflict does occur is generally not based on policy distinctions except in the most general terms (Welch and Bledsoe 1988).

Summary and Conclusions

Our "snapshot" of school board members in Texas offers few surprises. School board members tend to be middle-aged Anglo males who have graduated from college and enjoy relatively high incomes while working primarily in white-collar jobs. They have lived almost three decades in the communities they currently serve and have been school board members for almost five years.

Our survey of school board members indicates that there are significant differences between board members based on ethnicity and election structure. Anglo board members are more likely to have higher incomes and higher levels of education; they also are more likely to be conservative and to have a longer term of service on the school board (although the latter difference is not great). Mexican American board members are more likely to have lived longer in the community than their Anglo counterparts. Mexican American board members are more likely than Anglos to seek office for the purpose of serving their neighborhoods and in response to a concern over a particular issue.

In terms of electoral structure, board members elected from districts are less likely than those elected at-large to have high incomes, white-collar jobs, and college and postgraduate degrees. Mexican Americans are more likely than Anglos to be elected from districts, and district board members tend to have lived in the community longer and to have served on the school board for less time than at-large members. District board members are more likely than those elected at-large to seek office for the purpose of serving their neighborhoods and for the purpose of reacting to a single issue.

When we compare the responses to our survey by city council members with the responses by school board members, we find many similarities. This is not surprising, as both are significant local elective bodies. In addition, the change from at-large elections to district elections in both the city council and school board arenas often is in response to Voting Rights Act litigation (or the threat thereof); consequently, the remedy being sought also is similar, regardless of whether the governing body is a city council or a school board.

From a demographic standpoint, respondents to both surveys tend to be conservative Anglos about fifty years of age, who have white-collar jobs and have lived in their communities almost thirty years. They have served on their councils or school boards for almost five years.

Although the respondents are overwhelmingly male, a higher percent-age of females serve on school boards than serve on city councils, and although both groups are well educated and enjoy above-average in-comes, school board members are more likely to have a higher level of education and income.

When we examine differences based on ethnicity, again, both city council and school board respondents share some similarities. Mexican American council members and school board members are less well educated than Anglos and tend to have lived in their communities longer than Anglos. Mexican American elected officials are more likely than Anglos to view running for office as a way of increasing business contacts. And Mexican Americans on city councils and school boards also are more likely than Anglos to seek office in re-sponse to a concern over a particular issue. We did find some interest-ing intraethnic differences. Although Mexican American council members and school board members both are more likely to be conser-vative than liberal (as are Anglos), Mexican American school board members are much less conservative than their city council counter-parts. In addition, Mexican American council members are more likely than Mexican American school board members to view their current elected positions as stepping stones to higher office. This lack of politi-cal ambition on the part of ethnic school board members helps to support the notion of a school board that is politically apolitical (see Tucker and Zeigler 1977).

When we compare at-large council members and school board members with districted members, we again find common ground. Districted officials are more likely than at-large officials to have lived in their communities longer, but are likely to have served on their respective governing bodies for less time. And, as would be expected, representatives elected from districts are more likely than those elected at-large to identify service to the neighborhood as a motivating factor for seeking office.

Changing from at-large to district systems is viewed by the courts as a remedy for past discrimination against Mexican Americans. Conven-tional wisdom holds that district elections will enhance the chances of Mexican American candidates. Campbell and his colleagues (1985, 181) have noted the continuing increase in the number of minority school board members at the national level. Given the findings re-ported above, it seems safe to suggest that, as the number of minorities on school boards increases, a change in the role identification and behavior of school board members will also occur.

An equally important goal, one that goes beyond the symbolic gains of electoral victories and extends beyond passive representation, is to translate electoral victories into substantive policy changes for the Mexican American community. Tucker and Zeigler (1977, 11) argue that school boards are inefficient vehicles for citizens to use to influence educational policy. Our demonstration of significant differences between school board members, both demographically and in terms of representational foci, based on ethnicity and electoral form suggests that this is not necessarily the case.

Notes

1. Our questionnaire asked council members the form of electoral structure under which they were elected. "What type of election system is used in your community?" "If mixed, from what form were you elected?" We were able to isolate all council members elected from districts and those elected from at-large systems, including at-large representatives from mixed or hybrid systems. Thus, the conceptualization used in this analysis is on the individual level.

2. The form of our question was virtually identical to that of question 1 in the Welch and Bledsoe (1988) instrument: "We would like to know why you initially decided to seek election to the city/town council. Please rate the importance of each of the following factors in influencing your decision to run for a council seat. Circle best response."

3. The question was identical to the Welch and Bledsoe (1988) formulation: "Council members represent many different constituencies. In your own view, how important is your representation of each of the following constituencies?" Board members were asked to rate on a three-point scale.

4. The questions were: "Approximately how many hours per week do you devote to your job as a member of the school board?" and "Of the total number of hours per week, how many do you spend doing services for people?" As before, these questions were drawn from the Welch and Bledsoe (1988) survey. And, as before, we draw heavily upon the Welch and Bledsoe study and apply similar analyses to school boards.

6

Electoral Change and Policy Impacts in Cities

It is important to a minority community that minority candidates are elected to city councils where none had served before, if only for symbolic reasons. That is, we do not minimize the symbolic impact of a brown face where only white faces previously were found. But symbolism aside, if a Mexican American is elected to a city council, so what? Does the election of a Mexican American to a city council translate into substantive benefits for the Mexican American community? In virtually all ten cities in our study, following districting, Mexican Americans remained a numerical minority on the council, usually controlling only one vote of five. If districting is a remedy for the absence of representation, surely it must go beyond symbolism to be a remedy in more than name only.

Elections

In terms of the electoral impact, we ask three questions: Do more Mexican Americans run for office following districting? Do more Mexican American candidates win following districting? Are those who run and win following districting more likely to reside in predominantly Mexican American neighborhoods than prior to districting?

The latter concern speaks directly to the notion of minority representation. Ethnic underrepresentation may be a function not only of numbers but also of geography. That is, those minorities who are elected may not reside in or be representative of the minority residential areas of the city. We expect this pattern to change after districting. Under a district system, the council is apportioned among geographic

118

sections of a city. Where those cities already are divided between distinct ethnic and racial populations, and where each population lives in relatively segregated neighborhoods, the representatives of the districts would be more likely to reflect the dominant ethnic group of that district (see Lyons and Jewell 1988 and Zax 1990 for comments on residential segregation and electoral structure).

Thus, we look not only at overall representational equity but also at "residential equity"—that is, at how many Mexican American candidates actually reside in majority Mexican American neighborhoods.

In determining election equity, we defined the concept of more Mexican Americans running for council seats in terms of the candidate pool for each election. We calculated what percentage of all candidates for council seats were Mexican Americans. We also calculated the percentage of winning candidates who were Mexican Americans in each election. Since we used the general timeline of 1976–89 for this study, the number of elections before and after districting varies from city to city.

Representational equity is determined by dividing the percentage of Mexican Americans on the council by the percentage of Mexican Americans in the community. For example, an equity ratio of 1.00 would result if a city with a Mexican American population percentage of 33 percent had a city council whose composition were one-third Mexican American. We sum this equity score for each city and present an average for the years before and after the change to a district form of governance.

To determine "residential equity," we located the residential addresses of all Mexican American candidates for periods prior to the change to district elections and for all elections subsequent to districting. Utilizing census tract data, district demographic data, and expert testimony, we identified which candidates live in predominantly Anglo neighborhoods and which live in predominantly Mexican American neighborhoods, defined as those tracts with at least 60 percent Mexican American population. Where exact residential location could not be identified, we relied on the knowledge of local officials as to the ethnic composition of the neighborhood where the candidate resided. We examined the total number of candidates in each election, the total number of Mexican American candidates, the total number of Mexican American candidates who resided in Mexican American neighborhoods, and the total number of winning Mexican American candidates who resided in Mexican American neighborhoods.

Table 6.1 illustrates the increase in Mexican American candidates and electoral winners following districting as well as the representational equity scores. For purposes of our analyses, El Paso's postdistricting period follows redistricting completed in response to pressure from the Mexican American community. El Paso had changed its at-large system to districts sometime prior to such pressure, but, unlike the later districting, the earlier districts were drawn so as to minimize, not enhance, Mexican American political strength. As Table 6.1 indicates, in seven of the cities there were a rise in the percentage of Mexican Americans in the candidate pool and an increase in the percentage of winning candidates who were Mexican Americans. Two cities experienced no change, and one (San Antonio) saw a decrease.

All but one (El Paso) of our cities increased the representational equity score from predistricting to postdistricting (see Table 6.2, page 122). The average gain in representational equity is 0.36. What is especially noticeable is that several cities went from zero equity to nearly 50 percent equity. The largest representational equity gain occurred in the city (Lubbock) for which we have the highest residential segregation index score (0.63). This supports the findings of Vedlitz and Johnson (1982).

Taebel (1978) found that the size of the city council predicted minority representation. When we examined the larger councils in our sample, we found that the cities with larger councils had a representational equity gain of 0.25; the more common six-person-council cities had a representational equity gain of 0.41.

Electing more Mexican Americans to office may not be the only consequence of changing to single-member districts. We suggest that minority representatives who actually live in minority neighborhoods are likely to be a different type of representative from a minority group member who lives in the nonminority part of town. The history of Texas is replete with examples of "slating groups," which pick a token minority candidate, often from the Anglo part of town, to round out their slate. Therefore, we examined whether ethnic residential diversity increased after the shift to single-member districts.

We were able to collect the necessary residential data for eight of the ten cities (Beeville and El Paso are excepted). Table 6.3 (page 122) shows that the change from at-large to district elections results in changes in the residential areas from which Mexican American candidates either run and/or win.

In six of the eight cities, the change to districts resulted in a signifi-

Table 6.1

Candidates and Winners

	Running		Winners	
	Mexican American/All	%	Mexican American/All	%
Beeville				
Pre*	11/20	(0.55)	4/10	(0.40)
Post*	7/10	(0.70)	4/6	(0.66)
Big Spring				
Pre	1/11	(0.09)	0/5	(0.00)
Post	2/19	(0.10)	1/5	(0.20)
Corpus Christi[a]				
Pre	21/65	(0.32)	6/14	(0.43)
Post	21/60	(0.35)	6/14	(0.43)
El Paso				
Pre	31/84	(0.37)	6/21	(0.28)
Post	15/34	(0.44)	2/7	(0.28)
Lubbock				
Pre	4/25	(0.16)	0/6	(0.00)
Post	8/48	(0.17)	2/11	(0.18)
New Braunfels				
Pre	4/12	(0.33)	0/5	(0.00)
Post	3/8	(0.37)	2/4	(0.50)
Pleasanton				
Pre	3/10	(0.30)	0/6	(0.00)
Post	5/12	(0.42)	3/7	(0.43)
Port Lavaca				
Pre	3/16	(0.19)	1/9	(0.11)
Post	1/4	(0.25)	1/4	(0.25)
San Antonio[b]				
Pre	18/53	(0.34)	4/9	(0.44)
Post	46/130	(0.35)	11/33	(0.33)
Victoria				
Pre	1/23	(0.04)	0/10	(0.00)
Post	1/12	(0.08)	1/6	(0.17)

*Pre refers to predistricted elections, post to postdistricted elections. Years may vary.
[a]Some of the Corpus Christi data are from *Alonzo* v. *Jones*.
[b]The prior data for San Antonio are taken from Brischetto, Cotrell, and Stevens (1983).

cant increase in the number of Mexican American candidates who resided in Mexican American residential areas. In the two exceptions, Pleasanton and Corpus Christi, the same percentage of Mexican American candidates resided in the Mexican American neighborhoods under both at-large and district elections. However, in both of these communities, although the predistricting and postdistricting periods saw the same percentage of candidates residing in Mexican American neigh-

Table 6.2

Representational Equity

	Predistricting	Postdistricting
Beeville	0.55	0.95
Big Spring	0.00	0.58
Corpus Christi	0.60	0.70
El Paso	0.52	0.52
Lubbock	0.00	0.73
New Braunfels	0.00	0.41
Pleasanton	0.57	0.91
Port Lavaca	0.08	0.53
San Antonio	0.41	0.64
Victoria	0.00	0.41

Table 6.3

Neighborhood Equity: Percentage of Mexican American Candidates from Mexican American Neighborhoods

	Pre	Post
Beeville	100.0	100.0
Corpus Christi	68.0	68.0
Lubbock	22.2	62.5
Pleasanton	80.0	80.0
Victoria	0.0	75.0
San Antonio*	11.1	89.7
Port Lavaca	94.1	100.0
New Braunfels	0.0	50.0
Big Spring	0.0	33.3

*The prior data for San Antonio are taken from Brischetto, Cotrell, and Stevens (1983).

borhoods, the percentage of winning Mexican American candidates who lived in Mexican American neighborhoods rose following districting.

Indeed, in all cities for which we had available data, the percentage of winning Mexican American candidates living in Mexican American neighborhoods rose following districting (not reported in tabular form).

In addition to the empirical data, our discussions with the city managers of the cities confirmed that changing to districts increased the numbers of Mexican American candidates residing in predominantly

Mexican American neighborhoods and altered the perceived representational role of the council member. The city managers, including those who preferred at-large systems to districts, agreed that the newly elected Mexican American council members viewed their roles as directly representing the Mexican American neighborhoods, and that districting was a more representative system as the Mexican American community had a direct link to the council where none had existed before.

Overall, then, our data suggest that, following districting, Mexican Americans are more likely to run for office, more likely to win, and more likely to reside in predominantly Mexican American neighborhoods.

In part what we are saying is obvious. When district boundaries conform to neighborhoods characterized by ethnic homogeneity, those neighborhoods likely will elect members of their ethnic group to the city council. That this may be obvious does not impeach its significance: a change to district elections results in more minority candidates from minority residential neighborhoods and more winning minority candidates from minority neighborhoods.

Employment

There is a developing body of literature focusing on municipal employment, but less attention has been paid to municipal salary structures. As Browning, Marshall, and Tabb (1984) note, minority groups have traditionally used access to municipal employment as an important policy goal. Indeed, the success of the urban machine system was, in part, linked to its ability to provide municipal jobs for minority groups (Banfield and Wilson 1963). Today, almost a century after the rise of the reform movement, municipal employment remains important for minorities. The general question of minorities in the municipal work force has been extensively researched. Eisinger (1982) found that the African American percentage of a city's population was the best predictor of black representation in the municipal work force. Dye and Renick (1981) found that minority membership on a city council was an important determinant of minority percentage of municipal jobs, especially at the professional level. A comprehensive study by Mladenka (1989b, 173) found that, for total jobs, the black population percentage is the most significant predictor. For officials and administrators, however, Mladenka found that black representation on the city council is significant.

While most of the employment studies have focused on blacks, some studies have included Latinos (Browning, Marshall, and Tabb 1984; Karnig, Welch, and Eribes 1984; Mladenka 1989a, 1989b; Stein 1986). Both Browning, Marshall, and Tabb (1984) and Karnig, Welch, and Eribes (1984) found high correlations between Latino population percentage in the city and percentage of Latinos in municipal employment. Stein (1986) found that while the size of a city's minority population is the single most important explanatory factor, political and organizational arrangements also play significant roles. As Stein notes, "Not only do local political and organizational factors impact municipal hiring; they clearly do so in an interrelated fashion" (1986, 707). Mladenka found that, "Although the size of the minority population is the dominant factor in each of the regression equations, the level of political representation makes a difference" (1989a, 395).

We seek here to integrate descriptive representation studies with active representation. Previous work has indicated that form of electoral structure is an intervening variable, resulting in an expanded level of minority representation (Bullock and MacManus 1990; Davidson and Korbel 1981). In turn, then, minority representation should lead to greater minority employment. We test two hypotheses:

1. The greater the Mexican American population percentage, the greater the percentage of Mexican Americans in the municipal work force;
2. The greater the percentage of Mexican American members on the city council, the greater the Mexican American percentage of the municipal work force.

Our research focus is on the eight case study cities that meet two criteria: they have a population of at least 15 percent Spanish surname and have changed from at-large to some form of district elections for their city council within the past ten years. Due to the small number of cities on which our analysis is based, we use the city-year as our unit for analysis in a pooled cross-sectional design to increase the number of cases for analysis.

Our methodology closely follows that of Heilig and Mundt (1984) and Mladenka (1989a, 1989b). Our employment data are from EEO–4 forms furnished yearly by cities to the U.S. Equal Employment Opportunity Commission. These were collected from each of the eight cities. We use the 1976–86 period for our analyses.

In addition to the EEO–4 reports, we use longitudinal and cross-sectional data from city records, newspaper files, and the litigation files of MALDEF, Texas Rural Legal Aid, and the Southwest Voter Registration and Education Project.

Our independent variables are the percentage of the city population that is Mexican American, percentage of the city council that is Mexican American, percentage below poverty income, size of city, and type of electoral system, formulated as either districted (including mixed) or at-large systems.

Most of the studies cited above have focused on "gross" employment: that is, the total percentage of minorities in the municipal work force. As Stein (1986) notes, much of the minority employment in cities is at the lower end of the employment scale, in service and maintenance jobs (see also Dye and Renick 1981). We think it is important to see if districting and the subsequent increase in Mexican American percentage of city councils have an effect on the "status level" of their employment. Therefore, we examine relative employment at the upper end, middle, and lower end of the employment scale. This approach was suggested by the work of Stein and Condrey (1985).

Dye and Renick (1981) note that minority representation on a city council—that is, political representation—is the most influential variable affecting higher-status employment in a city work force. They also found that the mere presence of minority members on the council is important; it does not matter whether minority representation on the council corresponds to the minority percentage of the population. They go on to say that Latino employment in service jobs in cities does not require political representation. Employment in this category is generally a function of the size of the Latino population in the city (Dye and Renick 1981, 478). Stein and Condrey note, "In all cities, representation of minorities in the total workforce is better than in the categories of protective services, professionals or officials/administrators. It is in these categories where we clearly find the effects of political support, or lack thereof" (1985, 25). Mladenka (1989a, 395) notes that in the job categories of officials/administrators and professionals, the coefficients for mayor and council are higher than those for total jobs or for protective service.

One set of dependent variables, then, will be the percentage of employees at six different levels in the bureaucracy who are Mexican American.

We also examine employment by pay level. We develop the percentage of Mexican Americans employed in three pay levels as determined by the U.S. Equal Employment Opportunity Commission. We aggregate the pay categories into three levels: Low Pay comprises levels 1, 2, and 3 of the EEO–4 form; Middle Pay comprises levels 4, 5, and 6 of the form; High Pay comprises the top two pay grades. One reason for this manner of aggregation is that we look at a ten-year period, and, during that time frame, the dollar amounts per category shift. Therefore, we believe it is advisable to focus on an ordinal measure—low, middle, and high. We average the data for the predistricting and postdistricting periods.

We utilize an employment equity concept relating the percentage of Mexican American work force to the percentage of the population that is Mexican American. An equity score of 1.0 indicates that the percentage of Mexican Americans employed by the city is identical to the percentage of Mexican Americans in the population. We examine the average equity scores for the predistricting and postdistricting periods of the eight cities that filed EEO–4 reports.

As Table 6.4 indicates, the employment equity measure rose in four cities following redistricting and fell in four cities following redistricting. In the three cities with the largest percentage of Mexican American population (El Paso, San Antonio, and Corpus Christi) the equity scores rose following redistricting. However, none of the changes in either direction was dramatic.

As Dye and Renick (1981), Browning, Marshall, and Tabb (1984), and Stein (1986) note, an important measure of policy change is the distribution of minority employment within the city work force. That is, it is important to examine any effect redistricting may have on the status levels of Mexican American employment.

Traditionally, Mexican Americans have been concentrated in the lower-status, lower-paying jobs in a city work force. We examine what shifts, if any, occur in the distribution of the percentage of Mexican Americans at the various job levels following redistricting. We believe the initial impact of redistricting on municipal hiring patterns would most likely occur in the middle ranges of the employment hierarchy. There are fewer jobs at the top to distribute, and, as Browning, Marshall, and Tabb (1984, 195–96) note, there is likely to be more resistance from Anglos to redistribution at the top positions. At the same

Table 6.4

Employment Equity

	Percentage Hispanic	Percentage of City Work force Hispanic	Employment Equity
Big Spring			
Pre*	24.0	23.1	0.96
Post*	24.0	20.6	0.86
Corpus Christi			
Pre	47.0	37.8	0.80
Post	47.0	38.6	0.82
El Paso			
Pre	63.0	41.4	0.66
Post	63.0	42.6	0.68
Lubbock			
Pre	19.0	19.0	0.99
Post	19.0	20.0	1.05
New Braunfels			
Pre	34.0	34.0	1.02
Post	34.0	33.0	0.98
Port Lavaca			
Pre	45.0	28.0	0.63
Post	45.0	25.0	0.56
San Antonio			
Pre	54.0	37.0	0.69
Post	54.0	39.0	0.72
Victoria			
Pre	34.0	30.0	0.88
Post	34.0	29.0	0.85

*Pre refers to predistricted elections, post to postdistricted elections. Years may vary.

time, increases in hiring Mexican Americans at the lowest levels of the employment hierarchy following districting would not be likely to satisfy the various groups advocating the change to districting as a way of redressing the absence of representation for the Mexican American community. Consequently, we expect the policy impact to be reflected in the mid-levels of the municipal work force.

Our data support these expectations. The employment areas of greatest increases in Mexican American employment are those of office/clerical and protective service, with five cities reporting an increase in office clerical employment and six cities reporting an increase in protective service employment. The area of greatest decrease following districting is that of service/maintenance workers, with six of the cities reporting a decrease and only one reporting an increase. The change to a districted form of government enhances Mexican American employment at the middle level of employment and decreases it at the lower end of employment.

Karnig, Welch, and Eribes (1984) and Browning, Marshall, and Tabb (1984) did not find that political variables explained much of the variance in employment gains or losses. Dye and Renick (1981) noted a relationship between Mexican American employment and Mexican American representation on the city council. Much of the recent literature indicates that minority percentage of the population is the most effective predictor of overall minority municipal employment (Eisinger 1982; Mladenka 1989a 1989b; Stein 1986; Stein and Condrey 1985).

Our data support those findings (see Table 6.5). We found percentage of the population that is Mexican American to be a significant predictor in all but one of the six job areas. In addition, in all but one of the regressions estimating the individual job categories, in which the Mexican American population percentage was a significant predictor, a political variable, either the percentage of Mexicans on the city council or the form of government, was also significant. The one equation in which neither population nor political variables were significant was service employment, the lowest level of employment classification, with city size the significant predictor.

The data provided few surprises. The Mexican American percentage of the population generally was the most significant predictor. For the professional area of employment, as expected, the form of government, in addition to the Mexican American percentage of the population, was significant. For this employment category, the form of government variable was a negative 7.82, indicating that the percentage of Mexican American professionals employed was depressed in at-large cities. Thus, our findings support the literature that suggests that the minority percentage of the city population is the best predictor of minority employment in the city. Further, these data give limited support to the role that political variables such as the minority percentage on the city council and the form of government play in explaining Mexican American employment (see Dye and Renick 1981).

We remain somewhat tentative here, as other variables may contrib-

Table 6.5

Mexican American Employment

	Level of Employment					
	Administrative	Professional	Protective	Technical	Clerical	Service
% below poverty	-3.21	-1.32	-0.784	0.919	-0.993	-0.917
	(0.71)***	(1.16)	(1.05)	(0.627)	(0.695)	(1.10)
% council Mexican American	-0.037	-0.081	0.288	0.038	0.307	0.079
	(0.063)	(0.107)	(0.098)*	(0.061)	(0.064)***	(0.103)
% population Mexican American	0.657	1.12	0.919	0.712	0.559	0.187
	(0.123)***	(0.201)***	(0.19)***	(0.112)***	(0.121)***	(0.207)
Size of city (1,000s)	0.026	0.006	0.009	0.028	0.049	0.026
	(0.007)***	(0.012)	(0.01)	(0.007)***	(0.007)***	(0.001)**
Median family income	0.003	0.001	-0.000	0.001	-0.003	-0.001
	(0.001)***	(0.001)	(0.001)	(0.001)	(0.001)	(0.001)
Form of government	-0.265	-7.82	4.77	2.45	-0.576	5.42
	(2.19)	(3.73)*	(3.47)	(2.08)	(2.28)	(3.49)
Intercept	103.8	-16.3	-1.23	12.93	78.47	33.65
Adjusted R^2	0.69	0.56	0.65	0.83	0.91	0.38
F	21.05	12.17	18.13	59.86	92.11	6.63

Coefficients are regression coefficients (standard errors are in parentheses).
All equations except for technical workers were specified with an autoregressive term.

*$p < 0.05$.
**$p < 0.01$.
***$p < 0.000$.

ute to these changes. For example, we do not have relevant data on the educational levels of employees or on the pertinent seniority requirements within the city personnel regulations, all of which could play an important role in movement up or down the employment hierarchy. Nonetheless, the coefficients are in the direction we anticipated and, for the most part, support previous research (see, e.g., Mladenka 1989a, 1989b).

Pay Equity

As we have noted, we believe an increase in Mexican American employment characterized by hiring predominantly at the entry levels of the service and maintenance positions is not as significant as a change in the percentage of Mexican Americans hired at middle- and upper-status jobs, or as a change in the percentage of Mexican Americans receiving pay at the upper and middle categories. As with the status levels of employment, we expect that changes with the pay levels will more likely occur at the middle rather than upper levels.

We examined predistricting and postdistricting pay information for the cities. We established a pay equity concept by determining what percentage of the Mexican American work force was paid at low, middle, and high levels during the predistricting and postdistricting years. This is not a perfect method: extreme fluctuations in one year may unduly influence the average. We believe, however, that viewing the data this way provides insight into the significance of changing from at-large to district elections.

Table 6.6 reports pay equity. In all eight cities, the percentage of the Mexican American work force at either the middle or upper pay levels is higher during the period following districting than prior to districting. In all but one city (El Paso) the percentage of the Mexican American work force at the lowest pay level decreases. Districting, with its expanded Mexican American representation on city councils, results in an upward shift in Mexican American pay levels.

We further explored the changes in three regression equations for the percentage of Mexican Americans in the low, middle, and high pay categories. We used the same independent variables used for the employment status equations. Our dependent variable is the percentage of Mexican Americans in that pay category. The results are reported in Table 6.7 (page 132).[1] Our analysis resulted in significant equations

Table 6.6

Pay Equity: Mexican Americans as a Percentage of All Mexican Americans

	Low Pay	Middle Pay	High Pay
Big Spring			
Pre*	58.0	42.3	0.1
Post*	42.0	56.6	1.0
Corpus Christi			
Pre	39.7	55.8	4.7
Post	36.3	54.0	9.3
El Paso			
Pre	35.8	60.3	3.0
Post	40.0	56.3	3.3
Lubbock			
Pre	40.6	58.4	1.0
Post	27.0	71.0	2.0
New Braunfels			
Pre	70.2	29.7	0.0
Post	53.6	45.6	0.67
Port Lavaca			
Pre	61.0	37.7	1.3
Post	52.0	48.0	0.0
San Antonio			
Pre	53.3	40.0	6.6
Post	35.0	53.0	11.6
Victoria			
Pre	45.4	53.2	1.5
Post	42.5	56.0	1.2

* Pre refers to predistricted elections, post to postdistricted elections. Years may vary.

for pay level one and pay level three. Only one independent variable is significant for both equations—form of government. In the equation for pay level one, it is positive, indicating that at-large systems tend to have a greater percentage of the Mexican American work force at this pay level. In the equation for the upper pay levels, the variable is negative, indicating that for districted systems a greater percentage of the Mexican American work force is employed at those pay levels. For the highest pay level, size of the city is also a significant predictor.

We reestimated an equation for the middle-range pay equity, using only the form of government, size of city, and percentage of the population that is Mexican American. This reestimation produced a significant equation (Adjusted R^2 of 0.10/F of 3.75, $p < 0.05$), with size of city (0.00001/s.e. of 0.000006, significant at 0.05) and form of govern-

Table 6.7

Weighted Least Squares Estimates of Pay Equity

	Pay 1		Pay 2		Pay 3	
% below poverty	-0.128	(0.972)	0.458	(0.936)	0.029	(0.112)
% council Mexican American	0.037	(0.081)	0.016	(0.076)	0.021	(0.011)
% population Mexican American	0.275	(0.175)	-0.302	(0.170)	0.028	(0.022)
Size of city (1,000s)	-0.03	(0.0)	0.01	(0.09)	0.00	(0.001)*
Median family income	-0.001	(0.001)	0.0004	(0.001)	0.00	(0.00)
Form of government	8.17	(3.06)**	-6.09	(2.89)*	-2.35	(0.445)***
Intercept	64.9	(28.9)*	44.87	(27.8)	-4.2	(3.75)
R^2 (adj.)	0.24		0.06		0.65	
F	4.76		1.86 (ns)		22.08	

Coefficients are regression coefficients (standard errors in parentheses).

*$p < 0.05$.
**$p < 0.01$.
***$p < 0.000$.

ment (–6.16/s.e. of 2.82, significant at 0.05) both significant. The relatively large and negative unstandardized regression coefficient for the form-of-government variable indicates that districted forms of government enhance pay equity for level two.

Overall, then, our examination of the impact of districting and representational change on city employment policies suggests significant differences between the predistricting and postdistricting periods, with the postdistricting policies markedly more benevolent to Mexican American needs. Adding the analysis of the employment policies to that of the impact of districting on elections, we find that a change to districts increases the number of Mexican Americans on city councils, and that increased Mexican American representation has a modest effect on the distribution of Mexican American employment by the cities, while district systems have a more pronounced effect on the pay equity of Mexican American employees. Following districting, Mexican Americans are more likely to be employed at middle-level rather than lower-level municipal jobs and to be paid at somewhat higher levels than before districting.

Appointments

We turn now to the implications of representational change for city council decisions concerning appointments of Mexican Americans to city boards and commissions. Appointments to boards and commissions are important for three reasons. Traditionally, one of the significant pathways to elective local office has been prior service on local boards and commissions. Generally, appointments have also been a major means of rewarding supporters, and as Browning, Marshall, and Tabb (1984) note, of giving "at least symbolic representation" to groups. Finally, boards and commissions may have substantive impacts on the policy made by city councils. Clearly, then, appointment to boards and commissions is an important policy outcome for city councils.

Our dependent variable is the appointment of Mexican Americans to boards and commissions. The primary independent variable is the form of electoral system used by the city. Other independent variables include city population, Mexican American population percentage, percentage of Mexican American members on the council, and median income. Following Heilig and Mundt (1984), we use the term of the appointment as the unit of analysis for the measure. That is, each separate appointment, even if it is a reappointment, is counted. Unlike Heilig and Mundt, we count appointments for unexpired terms and subsequent reappointments as separate appointments. Browning, Marshall, and Tabb (1984) note that minority appointments can be concentrated in certain, perhaps unimportant or noninfluential commissions. Because of this, we selected for our analysis, with the assistance of key informants in each city, the four most important boards and commissions in each city. In this way, we hoped to gain a more accurate picture of actual "influential" appointments.

We create a measure of appointment equity by dividing the number of Mexican American appointments by the percentage of Mexican Americans in the population. If a city with 40 percent Mexican American population appointed Mexican Americans as 40 percent of its appointments to significant boards and commissions, then the equity score for that city would be 1.00. We summed and averaged the equity scores for the predistricting and postdistricting periods. These data are reported in Table 6.8.

Table 6.8 reveals that the postdistricting appointment equity scores rose in seven of the nine cities for which we have data. The general predistricting average equity score was 0.45, and the postdistricting equity score was 0.61. While this represents a significant overall gain, the individual gains were as low as 0.03 and as high as 0.74. In only one city (Big Spring) does the Mexican American equity score rise above 1.00.

To ascertain greater explanation of the appointment equity, we performed a multiple regression analysis utilizing the equity score as the dependent variable. As before, we utilize the city-year as our case for analysis. In that way, we increase the number of cases for our inquiry. Our independent variables included the Mexican American percentage of the population, form of government, median family income of the city, and percentage of the city council that was Mexican American. Our estimated regression equation is reported in Table 6.9.

The equation was significant and had two variables: Mexican American percentage of the city population ($t = 3.174$/significance = 0.01; $b = 0.276$) and Mexican American percentage of the city council ($t = 3.570$/significance = 0.000; $b = 0.378$) as significant estimators of the appointment equity scores. We also estimated a reduced-model equation using only the Mexican American percentage of city population and Mexican American percentage on the city council. The reduced-model equation is presented in Table 6.10 (page 136).

Table 6.8

Appointment Equity

	Predistricting	Postdistricting
Beeville	0.64 (3 years)	0.85 (6 years)
Big Spring	0.31 (7 years)	1.05 (2 years)
Corpus Christi	0.58 (7 years)	0.63 (3 years)
El Paso	0.49 (6 years)	0.44 (4 years)
Lubbock	0.52 (8 years)	0.73 (2 years)
New Braunfels	0.30 (4 years)	0.54 (3 years)
Pleasanton	N/A	N/A
Port Lavaca	0.39 (8 years)	0.30 (2 years)
San Antonio	0.59 (2 years)	0.75 (8 years)
Victoria	0.28 (5 years)	0.31 (5 years)

Table 6.9

Appointment Equity: Regression Equation

Independent Variable	Regression Coefficients	T
Median family income	−0.0007	−1.29
Electoral structure	−3.82	−1.65
% population Mexican American	0.276**	3.174
% city council Mexican American	0.378***	3.570

$R^2 = 0.46$; $F = 18.53$; significance $= 0.000$; $N = 72$.
   **Significant at 0.01.
   ***Significant at 0.000.

Table 6.10

Appointment Equity: Reduced Model

Independent Variable	Regression Coefficients	T
% population Mexican American	0.316***	3.65
% city council Mexican American	0.447***	4.32

$R^2 = 0.44$; $F = 33.16$; significance = 0.000; intercept = 2.7; cases = 72.
***Significant at 0.000.

Both coefficients are significant. A 1 percent change in the percentage of city council members who are Mexican American has a stronger impact on board appointments than a 1 percent change in the percentage of the city population that is Mexican American. Using these estimated coefficients, we find that a city with a low percentage of Mexican Americans in the population (20 percent) and a Mexican American percentage on the city council of 10 percent would have an appointment equity score of 0.13. A high Mexican American population city (60 percent) with a large share of the city council Mexican American (50 percent) would have an estimated appointment equity score of 0.43. Even in those cities with large Mexican American populations and a hefty share of the city council, the appointment equity score lags.

Our multivariate tests indicate that Mexican Americans are consistently underrepresented on important boards and commissions. Our findings generally are consistent with those of Browning, Marshall, and Tabb (1984). However, unlike our study, Browning, Marshall, and Tabb found that appointment equity was roughly equal to level of representation on the city council. Our study found that form of governmental structure—that is, at-large or district—is not as important as (1) Mexican American percentage of the city council and (2) percentage of the city population that is Mexican American.

At the same time, form of government obviously is an intervening variable, producing more Mexican Americans on the city council. Given that appointment to boards and commissions is one of the traditional pathways to elective local office, to the extent that cities underrepresent Mexican Americans on significant boards and commissions, it is not surprising that successful Mexican American political candidacies also lagged. However, changing from at-large to district systems has helped produce more Mexican American candidacies and more Mexican American winners and thus more Mexican American appointments to important boards and commissions.

Summary

We return to the question posed at the beginning of this chapter. Does it make any difference to the Mexican American community if district elections replace at-large elections? Our data support the conclusion that substantial differences occur not only in the electoral arena but also in the policy arena.

We find that under district systems, more Mexican American candidates seek and win office. Importantly, we find also that winning Mexican American candidates are more likely to come from Mexican American neighborhoods. Further, we find that after winning, the presence of Mexican Americans on the city council influences the policy decisions of the council in the areas of municipal employment, municipal salaries, and the appointment of Mexican Americans to city boards and commissions. Following districting, more Mexican Americans are hired in the higher ranks of municipal employees, and more Mexican Americans enjoy higher pay status. Finally, more Mexican Americans are appointed to the important municipal boards and commissions.

Note

1. An examination of the ordinary least squares regressions revealed that errors for the regressions were heteroscedastic, or nonconstant. As a result, OLS estimates for these equations are not robust (Berry and Feldman 1985, 77). To overcome these problems and provide estimates that are more robust, we apply iterative weighted least squares (Krasker 1988; Rubin 1983). Specifically, we used the sine estimates approach of David Andrews (1974, 523), which generates coefficients that are "resistant to gross deviations of a small measure of points and relatively efficient over a broad range of distributions." When the data meet the error assumptions of ordinary least squares, this technique produces estimates identical to the ordinary least squares estimates.

7

Electoral Change and Policy Impacts in Schools

The Politics of Mexican American Education

The politics of Mexican American education in Texas are a microcosm of minority education in the nation, replete with instances of ethnic prejudice. Weinberg (1977, 5) argues that the educational history of minority children in the United States is marked by certain common characteristics:

1. The minority community and families occupy a subordinate position in American society.
2. Excluded from having a voice in government, members of the minority community find public institutions closed to them or available only on a limited basis.
3. Because of their position of relative powerlessness, members of the minority community are forced (taxed) to pay for institutions that they cannot enjoy.
4. Educational institutions adopt the prevailing social evaluation of the minority group and only grudgingly fit its members into the institutions.
5. The dominant society denies the cultural distinctiveness of the minority group.

All of these characteristics describe the history of Mexican American education in Texas. There has been an official denial of Mexican American heritage, including prohibition of the speaking of Spanish while in school. As Friedman put it, "The schools functioned as an

138

agency of assimilation: The Anglos, who set the policy, attempted to inculcate their values, ideas, beliefs, language and history upon the Mexican Americans" (1978, 227).

The public education system of Texas developed very slowly from the period of the Texas Revolution (1836) through Reconstruction. In fact, one of the grievances that the Texas rebels had against Mexico was the lack of a public educational system. Following independence, the state was slow to develop an educational system and even slower to incorporate Mexican Americans into it. Mexican American children were shut out of the developing Texas educational system, and there is little evidence of substantial enrollment of Mexican American students before the beginning of the twentieth century (Friedman 1978; Weinberg 1977).

Once Mexican American students began enrolling in public schools, they still faced in-school discrimination. As Weinberg notes, "By 1920, a pattern had emerged for Texas as a whole: separate schooling in greatly inferior facilities for Mexican Americans; deliberate refusal to make educational use of the child's cultural heritage, especially the Spanish language, and a shorter school year" (1977, 145).

The creation of "Mexican Schools" in Mexican American neighborhoods also was common. Manuel (1930, 59) describes one situation:

> In a small town in North Central Texas a rural district maintains a four teacher school for other white children and one block away a Mexican school. The latter is housed in a room about 20 feet by 20 feet. The enrollment at the time of the writer's visit was 38, and 30 were in regular attendance. These children are given a 5-month's school—such as it is—while the other school has a term of 8 months. (1930, 59)

We noted in our earlier description of Big Spring that, in 1931, the school board authorized the construction of a school for "Mexicans," but ordered it closed during "cotton-picking season" so the schoolchildren could work in the fields. By the early 1940s, "Mexican Schools" existed in 122 school districts in fifty-nine Texas counties (Allsup 1982, 26).

This segregation of Mexican Americans in Texas public schools was declared unconstitutional in *Delgado* v. *Bastrop Independent School District* in 1948. Judge Rice said:

> The regulations, customs, usages and practices of the defendants . . .
> have segregated pupils of Mexican or other Latin American descent in
> separate classes and schools. . . . [They] are, and each of them is, arbi-
> trary and discriminatory and in violation of plaintiff's constitutional
> rights as guaranteed by the Fourteenth Amendment to the Constitution
> of the United States, and are illegal. (Quoted in San Miguel 1982, 704)

However, neither *Delgado* nor *Brown* v. *Board of Education* eliminated segregated schools for Mexican Americans in Texas. Mexican
American students continued to face various forms of de facto segregation, including "Mexican rooms" in Anglo schools (see San Miguel
1982). And the traditional practice of residential segregation facilitated
the placement of Mexican American children in Mexican American
neighborhood schools.

Participation by Mexican Americans in
Educational Politics

Effective participation by the Mexican American community in the
educational decision-making process did not take place in the first few
decades of the twentieth century (San Miguel 1979, 58). During the
1930s, Mexican Americans and Mexican American organizations attempted to eliminate the segregation of Mexican American children in
Texas schools (San Miguel 1979). San Miguel argues that during the
period of 1930–1960, a "politics of persuasion," relying on a wide
range of tactics designed to alter the status quo, prevailed. The Mexican American community, working through such ethnic organizations
as the League for United Latin American Citizens (LULAC) and the
American G.I. Forum, sought redress of grievances with the educational establishment (1979, 117–18). LULAC, perhaps the best-known
organization focusing on Mexican American empowerment, was
formed in the 1920s in Corpus Christi, Texas. The G.I. Forum was
developed following World War II to secure rights for returning Mexican American veterans, but became involved in broader issues facing
Mexican American communities during the postwar period. Despite
the efforts of these organizations and others, the Anglo establishment
remained dominant and largely unmoved.

The development in Texas of effective Mexican American political
participation in educational politics centered on two main themes: a

focus on local elections and the mobilization of such organizations as *La Raza Unida* party, LULAC, the American G.I. Forum, the Mexican American Legal Defense and Education Fund (MALDEF), and Mexican American Democrats (MAD). Pierce and Hagstrom say:

> Hispanics have made significant gains in state and local elections—either with particularly attractive candidates or in areas where their numbers were so large that it was not necessary to seek support from the mainstream of society. The Southwest [voter registration] project has concentrated its registration efforts on local races in the belief that most critical issues facing Mexican Americans—education and street and sanitation improvements in long neglected neighborhoods—are decided locally. (1988, 15)

From the 1960s to the 1980s, the "politics of persuasion" used a variety of strategies and tactics, principally focusing on litigation. This was especially true following the creation of MALDEF (O'Connor and Epstein 1984).

In 1970, a federal district court held in *Cisneros v. Corpus Christi Independent School District* that Mexican Americans were an identifiable sociological minority and that they had been victimized by de jure segregation (Rangel and Alcala 1972; San Miguel 1987). After a complicated appeals process, the U.S. Supreme Court upheld the finding (San Miguel 1987, 181).

In Texas, the urban reform education model, using at-large electoral systems and nonpartisan ballots and setting election dates at times when no partisan election would be held, was in place when Mexican American empowerment organizations turned to the issue of education. The initial focuses of their campaign were on eliminating the segregation of Mexican American children, improving bilingual education programs, and developing a curriculum more sensitive to Mexican American needs. By the early 1980s, only minimal progress had been made in these areas (San Miguel 1987, 216–17).

Among the reasons for the failure of the Mexican American community to reach its goals fully were misplaced strategies. San Miguel notes:

> Mexican Americans made three fundamental errors. First, they concentrated on influencing educational policies rather than on replacing educational policymakers and the governance structures facilitating their

> actions. Second, their challenges to discrimination focused almost ex-
> clusively on administrative practices. . . . Third, Mexican Americans
> failed to identify and eliminate the root cause of educational inequality:
> the opposition by local school officials. (1987, 217)

We share San Miguel's view of the intertwining of politics, bureaucracy, and educational policy making. Central to the creation of policies favorable to Mexican Americans is the creation of governance
structures that facilitate the election of Mexican Americans to school
boards. One view would anticipate that those elected policy makers
would intervene directly in the distribution of services to ameliorate
conditions for the Mexican American community (Meier, Stewart, and
England 1991). For educational policies, however, the process is somewhat more involved. Favorable governance structures facilitate the
election of Mexican Americans to the school board, who in turn hire
Mexican American administrators, and the administrators then hire
Mexican American teachers. In effect, then, the process begins with
the creation of a governance structure that facilitates the election of
Mexican Americans and leads to increased Mexican American representation in the educational bureaucracy.

The favorable electoral structure is some form of district election.
When local school boards change from at-large schemes to district
elections, minority representation on those school boards increases.
Mexican Americans elected to school boards serve not only as representatives of the community, but also as symbolic examples of political
gain. The general ethnic politics literature notes that having co-ethnics
in positions of authority is important in and of itself. Minority persons
apparently "feel" better represented when a co-ethnic is representing them (Browning, Marshall, and Tabb 1984; Welch and Bledsoe
1988, 110).

The change in election structure, however, is most important because of the consequent policy changes implemented through the educational bureaucracy. By the early 1980s, MALDEF, Texas Rural
Legal Aid, and the Southwest Voter Education Project were busily
pursuing the creation of safe electoral districts for Mexican Americans,
using the Voting Rights Act to coerce removal of at-large systems
from school boards in those areas with at least 20 percent Mexican
American population. We turn now to an examination of the results of
that strategy.

Methodology

We apply the expanded political resources model discussed in chapter 1 to school boards. Our dependent variables include "second-generation discrimination" measures (Bullock and Stewart 1978; Meier and Stewart 1991; Meier, Stewart, and England 1989). These include the Mexican American student graduation rates, the suspension rates of Mexican American students, and the assignment of students to bilingual programs, gifted and talented (GT) programs, and educably mentally retarded (EMR) programs. GT, EMR, and bilingual programs generally fall into the category of ability grouping. That is, these three areas are filled by students chosen because of specific ability characteristics. We also use the percentage of the school district with a high school education as one of the political resource variables. These are policies that affect the access of minority students to educational resources, even though the schools are, in theory, integrated. Some call them "in-school" segregation (see Meier, Stewart, and England 1989, 40–58).[1]

The differential placement of students in ability-grouping classes affects their access to educational resources. Previous research has indicated that minority students are more likely to be assigned to lower-level academic groups (Heller, Holtzman, and Messick 1982; Meier, Stewart, and England 1989). EMR class assignments are potentially the most subject to discrimination (Meier and Stewart, 1991, 127). On the other hand, assignment to GT classes is a positive outcome for the student. Traditionally, these classes attract the best teachers and often have small class sizes. Some classes carry extra weight for the calculation of student GPA and class standing.

Assignment to bilingual classes is somewhat different. As early as the 1930s, bilingual education was seen as a problem area for education in the Southwest (Manuel 1930; Sanchez 1934). Today, bilingual education remains a controversial political issue. Conflicting research findings concerning the efficacy of bilingual instruction continue to stir the political waters. Our concern here is with the use of bilingual programs in a disproportionate manner. Following Meier and Stewart (1991), we consider bilingual classes for their impact on the segregation of Mexican American and Anglo children. That is, we identify bilingual classes as a form of discrimination against Mexican American children, as they are used frequently as a way of "tracking" lower-achievement children, resulting often in de facto segregated classes.

Disciplinary measures include suspensions and expulsions. While all schools must maintain discipline within the confines of the school, disciplinary practices that are applied in such a way that they selectively punish poor or minority children become measures of second-generation discrimination. Suspending or expelling students on the basis of their minority status obviously denies them access to educational resources.

Because previous research (Robinson, England, and Meier 1985) has found no significant differences between ward and mixed systems, we treat them together. We lag system with other variables; that is, we use system as measured in 1984 with our other variables measured in 1986 for both theoretical and practical reasons. Theoretically, school board members need time on the board to have an impact. As a practical matter, some systems changed from at-large to districted election structure after elections had been held for that year. Thus, to avoid misspecification, we lag the system. The variables are operationalized as follows: electoral system as 0 for at-large and 1 for districted systems.

Our dependent variables are essentially the same as those of Meier and Stewart (1991). We use ratios to measure the impact of minority representation on such categories as ability grouping, student disciplinary actions, and educational attainment. In the first category, ability grouping, we include the number of students assigned to bilingual programs, the number of students assigned to classes for the educable mentally retarded (EMR), and the number of students assigned to gifted and talented programs. For each grouping, we use a "representational ratio" or equity score. The ratio is calculated by dividing the proportion of Mexican American students in the grouping by the proportion of Mexican American students in the school district.[2] The ratio would equal 1.0 when Mexican Americans have access to the grouping in exact proportion to their overall numbers. Ratios above 1.0 indicate that a greater proportion of Mexican Americans are in the grouping than the proportion they constitute of the student body, while ratios below 1.0 indicate proportionally fewer Mexican Americans in the group.

We include sixty-four Texas school districts in our inquiry, with a time frame of 1976 to 1986. We chose a ten-year period to establish a longitudinal base. We chose this particular ten-year period because it marked a peak of activity in Texas with respect to changes from at-large to districting systems.

School district surveys conducted by the Office for Civil Rights (OCR) in the Department of Education furnish much of the data used in our study. In addition to OCR data, we use data from the Texas Education Agency and the Texas Association of School Boards (TASB).

We used TASB data to identify all the Independent School Districts (ISDs) in Texas that had changed from at-large to district systems. The original number of such districts was thirty-two. Our requirement that at least 5 percent of the district's population be Mexican American, combined with errors found in the TASB data, made it impossible to examine all thirty-two districts for each of the ten years within our time frame. For most of the years in our analysis, the number of districted school districts ranged from eighteen to twenty-eight.

Initially, we matched our target group of thirty-two school districts with a control group of thirty-two at-large systems. The matching was based on the size of the district, percentage of minority population, and region of state. Some of these control districts changed their electoral structure while our research was ongoing, and one district merged with another, reducing the actual number of control districts to twenty-seven. We used both path analysis and regression analysis to examine our data.

The Creation of Electoral Structure

The "unreforming" of electoral structures in Texas has been a long and slow process. Largely in response to litigation, Texas schools slowly began to change their electoral structure throughout the 1980s. Although no precise number exists, prior to 1970 there were fewer than fifteen school districts in Texas using some form of district electoral structure. By the mid-1980s thirty-six school districts were using district elections. We constructed an equation that would predict adoption of a districted form of government. Since the dependent variable is dichotomous, the proper analytical technique is a form of log-linear analysis. We chose logistic regression, using the SPSS system. We estimated an equation using the full expanded political resources model discussed in chapter 1. Because of multicollinearity problems, the equation included no significant predictors.[3] We reestimated the equation utilizing Mexican American percentage of the population and whether or not litigation was involved in the change to a district form of electoral structure.[4] The findings are reported in Table 7.1.

Table 7.1

Districted Form of Election Structure

Independent Variables	b	Standard Error
% Hispanic population	0.0271*	0.014
Litigation	11.49	37.82

Percentage of cases correctly classified = 82.46; model chi-square = 38.3; DF 2; significance: $p < 0.000$.
*$p < 0.10$.

Table 7.2

Mexican American School Board Seats as a Function of Mexican American Population

	b	Standard Error
% population Mexican American	0.788*	0.077

R^2 (adj.) = 0.620; F 102.3; significance: $p < 0.000$; intercept = –2.05.
*$p < 0.000$.

Table 7.1 identifies the percentage of Hispanic population as the only significant variable. This is not surprising, since perhaps the single most significant political resource available to a minority population is its share of the total population. Our litigation measure may be obscured by the impact of the threat of litigation, especially when a nearby jurisdiction has lost a case, often having to pay significant litigation costs. We also estimated an equation regressing the percentage of Mexican American school board seats on the percentage of Mexican Americans in the population. Table 7.2 reports that the percentage Mexican American in the population does not fully translate into school board seats.

With a negative intercept, and a slope of less than 1.0, the Mexican American population will not receive a proportionate share of school board seats. A Mexican American population percentage of 60 translates into approximately 45 percent of the school board seats. These data are compatible with those of Meier and Stewart (1991, 92), who found that a 60 percent Hispanic population would receive 47 percent of school board seats.

Electoral Structure and Mexican American Representation

In addition to population, electoral structure has a major effect on representation (Engstrom and McDonald 1982; Meier and Stewart 1991). However, the electoral system may not, by itself, drive minority representation; rather, it must be viewed as an interactive measure whose effect will be less a function of a direct relationship between structure and minority representation and more a function of how the structure interacts with such other variables as minority share of the population.[5]

We estimated two equations, first using the interactive term with two other political resources of the Mexican American community and then one with the interactive terms only. These data are presented in Tables 7.3 and 7.4.

As can be seen in Table 7.3, the two significant variables are electoral structure and population. What is of interest is the closeness of these two structural variables. Both are positive, and although the districted variable is somewhat higher, the at-large variable is fairly close. Meier and Stewart suggest that the at-large system has a greater negative impact on the Hispanic community when Hispanics are not a significant voting constituency. They argue that, for school district elections, turnout is likely to be a function of having children in the school system. With a small population percentage, Hispanics can become an "implied" voting majority in school board elections (Meier and Stewart 1991, 97). Meier and Stewart estimate that with as low as 38 percent of the total school district population, Hispanics can account for 50 percent of the student enrollment (see their Table 4.5, p. 97). We estimate a similar equation, and our results (Table 7.5) closely match their data.

We estimate that Mexican Americans can become an "implied" voting majority at 40 percent of the population. We then reestimate equation 7.3 for those districts with less than 40 percent Mexican American population.

Our data suggest that the impact of both at-large and districting schemes is more muted when Mexican Americans are in a clear minority. Meier and Stewart (1991, 97) found that the impact of at-large

Table 7.3

**Mexican American School Board Seats as a Function of
Electoral Structure and Political Resources**

Independent Variable	b	Standard Error
District x Mexican American population	0.780***	0.110
At-Large x Mexican American population	0.754***	0.088
Mexican American–Anglo income ratio	–0.226	0.431
Mexican American education	0.591	0.554

R^2 (adj.) = 0.59; F = 23.5; significance: $p < 0.000$; intercept = -8.88.
***$p < 0.000$.

Table 7.4

**Mexican American School Board Seats as a Function of
Electoral Structure**

	b	Standard Error
District form	0.786***	0.087
At-large form	0.746***	0.110

R^2 (adj.) = 0.593; F = 46.27; significance: $p < 0.000$; intercept = -4.42.
***$p < 0.000$.

elections were much more severe. For our data, when Mexican Americans are in a minority, they are clearly better served by district elections.

Electoral Structure, Bureaucracy, and Mexican American Representation

Administrators

Much of the literature on representative bureaucracy has centered on the question of the representation of minorities in bureaucratic positions (see discussion in chapter 5). Generally, this literature has found that minorities are in positions at the low end of the bureaucratic hierarchy, where they exercise less influence over decision making. Meier

Table 7.5

Percentage of Mexican American Students as a Function of Mexican American Population

	b	Standard Error
% population Mexican American	1.14***	0.051

R^2 (adj.) = 0.889; F = 499; significance: $p < 0.000$; intercept = 4.506.
***$p < 0.0001$.

Table 7.6

Mexican American School Board Seats as a Function of Electoral Structure and Political Resources (Mexican American population less than 40 percent)

Independent Variable	b	Standard Error
District x Mexican American population	0.533***	0.128
At-Large x Mexican American population	0.273*	0.143
Mexican American–Anglo income ratio	–0.716	3.178
Mexican American education	0.306	0.375

R^2 (adj.) = 0.23; F = 4.75; significance: $p < 0.0036$; intercept = –1.69.
*$p < 0.10$.
***$p < 0.000$.

---

and Stewart (1991, 107) found that Mexican Americans were significantly underrepresented at the administrator level within school systems. The process of hiring minority school administrators, a function of school boards, essentially is a political one and should be linked to the political resources available to the minority community. We suggest that the percentage of Mexican Americans on a school board should significantly affect the hiring of Mexican American administrators in that school district. For example, Mladenka (1989a, 395) found that for job categories at the upper end of the scale—that is, officials/administrators and professionals—the coefficients for mayor and council are higher than those for total jobs or for lower-level jobs. Stein and Condrey (1985, 25) note that the representation of minorities in the total work force is better than in the category of professionals or

Table 7.7

**Percentage of Mexican American Administrators as a
Function of Political Resources**

Model Independent Variables	Full Model	Reduced
% population Mexican American	0.299*	0.320*
	(0.097)	(0.096)
% school board Mexican American	0.465***	0.451***
	(0.097)	(0.096)
Mexican American education	−30.7	—
	(17.7)	
Mexican American–Anglo income ratio	4.35	—
	(3.27)	
R^2 (adj.)	0.72	0.71
F	40.77	76.6
Significance	$p < 0.000$	$p < 0.000$
Intercept	2.44	−1.19

*$p < 0.05$.
***$p < 0.000$.

officials/administrators, and it is in those categories that the effects of political support are found. These findings are supported by Dye and Renick (1981), who found that minority representation on a city council—that is, political representation—is the most influential variable affecting higher-status employment.

We estimated an equation using the political resources model and including percentage of the population that is Mexican American, the percentage of Mexican Americans on the school board, the percentage of the school district population with a high school education, and the Mexican American–Anglo income ratio. The results are in Table 7.7.

This model predicts the percentage of Mexican American administrators in a district. Two of the four variables, population and percentage of Mexican Americans on the school board, are statistically significant. These are the same variables Meier and Stewart found to be significant. In our study, the regression coefficient for school board membership is somewhat larger and has a higher ratio of coefficient to standard error than does the coefficient for population.[6] That is, we found Mexican American representation on the school board to be somewhat more important than in previous studies. For every one-point increase in the percentage of Mexican Americans on the school board, there is almost a one-half-point increase in the percentage of Mexican American administrators.

When we estimated an equation for the reduced model (see Table 7.6), our results resemble those of Meier and Stewart and are consistent with those of the full model. Again, it is the percentage of Mexican Americans on the school board that leads the way in predicting Mexican American representation at the high end of the educational bureaucracy.

Teachers

Minorities are more likely to be represented at the lower levels of the bureaucratic system (see Dye and Renick 1981; Mladenka 1989a, 1989b; Stein 1986). Minorities also are more likely to be teachers than administrators in a given school district. Meier and Stewart (1991, 108) characterize teachers as "implementation bureaucrats" in the educational system. Such individuals are likely to be the ones who exercise administrative discretion in carrying out their duties (see Lipsky 1980). We estimated an equation attempting to predict the percentage of Mexican American teachers in the school district, using the same variables as in Table 7.7, with the addition of percentage of Mexican American administrators. The results are presented in Table 7.8.

The model accurately predicts the percentage of Mexican American teachers, accounting for 90 percent of the variation. Four of the variables in the model are significant. As expected, the percentage of Mexican Americans in the population and percentage of Mexican American administrators in the school district are significant. Clearly, Mexican American administrators play a vital role in the process of bringing Mexican American teachers into the district. Our findings are similar to the findings of Meier and Stewart. Our results, however, indicate a stronger relationship than Meier and Stewart found between the percentage of Mexican American teachers and the percentage of the school district population with a high school education. What might be at work here is the process of recruitment. An educated population may be a prerequisite for having qualified Mexican American college graduates. The coefficients indicate that for every one-percentage-point increase in the Mexican American population with a high school education, there is a 0.297-point increase in the percentage of Mexican American teachers. The pattern remains essentially the same after we estimate a reduced-model equation. Unlike Meier and Stewart, we found

Table 7.8

Percentage of Mexican American Teachers as a Function of Political Resources

Model Independent Variables	Full Model	Reduced
% population Mexican American	0.281**	0.283**
	(0.053)	(0.052)
% school board Mexican American	0.129*	0.129*
	(0.058)	(0.057)
Mexican American education	0.297**	0.293**
	(0.093)	(0.091)
Mexican American–Anglo income ratio	−4.51	—
	(1.69)	
% administrators Mexican American	0.419***	0.416***
	(0.066)	(0.065)
R^2 (adj.)	0.90	0.90
F	117.4	149.1
Significance	$p < 0.000$	$p < 0.000$
Intercept	8.74	−8.97

   * $p < 0.05$.
  ** $p < 0.01$.
 *** $p < 0.000$.

Mexican American representation on the school boards to be significant. This may be a reflection of the size variation in the districts we examined. Our analyses included both large and small districts, whereas Meier and Stewart concentrated solely on large districts. This suggests that there is a different political dynamic at work when one examines school districts of different sizes. In small districts, for example, the impact of minority political pressure may be more concentrated than in large districts where minority support may be more diffuse. The results of political pressure in a small district may also be more visible where one is dealing with fewer schools; this visibility may have a direct impact on the accountability of an elected school board member that would not be so evident in large districts.

Electoral Structure and Second-Generation Discrimination

In an attempt to explain more fully the interrelationships between electoral structure and policies of second-generation discrimination, we present a hypothesized model to examine second-generation discrimination among Mexican American schoolchildren. We posit form of electoral structure as the prior variable in a path analysis model. The problem posed by at-large elections is obvious. Since the minority group is a numerical as well as a sociological minority, it will be at a disadvantage if it must attract a majority of votes from an entire school district, rather than from a more compact, single-member district in which the minority group constitutes a majority of the single-member district's population.

Following districting, more Mexican Americans should win seats on the school board. We then expect that increased numbers of Mexican Americans on a school board will increase the number of Mexican American administrators, as we have found above. Indeed, Meier, Stewart, and England (1991, 162–63) contend that education is more susceptible to administrative influence than other policy areas are, thus accenting the importance of having Mexican Americans on the governing body of a school district. Put another way, the hiring of school administrators is part of a political process; we expect the presence of Mexican American school board members to influence that political dynamic and to result in the increased employment of Mexican American administrators.

The increase in the number of Mexican American administrators should lead to increased numbers of Mexican American teachers in the school district. As we reported above, our data support this assumption.

Finally, our hypothesized model posits that the increase in Mexican American teachers will limit second-generation discrimination found in the school district. Heller, Holtzman, and Messick (1982, 38) indicate that classroom teachers are the educational constituency most likely to influence policies regarding equal access to education. The educational literature establishes that teachers have a substantial impact on student performance (Brophy 1983). Meier and Stewart (1991, 28) suggest that Latino teachers can have an impact on Latino students simply by serving as role models in the classroom. We examine this impact with respect to selected second-generation discrimination variables.

The hypothesized model also posits that increased numbers of Mexican American teachers will correlate positively with such successful academic activities as numbers of Mexican American students enrolled in GT programs and the number of Mexican American students who graduate from high school. Further, the model suggests a negative relationship between the number of Mexican American teachers and such policy areas as assignments to bilingual classes, EMR classes,

Table 7.9

Education Policy Ratios by Ethnicity (1986)

Policy Ratio	Mexican Americans	Anglos
Bilingual	3.67*	0.050
Suspensions	1.00	0.970
EMR classes	1.04*	0.710
Gifted and talented	0.47*	1.97
Graduates	0.74*	1.30
Teacher ratio	0.70*	2.40
Administrator ratio	0.86*	2.23

*Significantly different from Anglos at 0.01 level.

and such disciplinary measures as suspensions.

In addition to the path analysis model, we extend our analyses by the use of regression. Meier and Stewart (1989, 37) have noted an interactive effect on second-generation discrimination variables between Mexican American school board members and Mexican American teachers. We also examine the impact of this interactive variable. The percentage of Mexican American teachers is multiplied by the percentage of Mexican American board members. Then, the square root of the product is taken in order to translate the measure into a percentile figure.

Table 7.9 presents the mean policy ratios by ethnicity of student. In 1986, Mexican American students were underrepresented in the positive categories of GT programs, graduates, teacher ratio, and administrator ratio. Mexican Americans were overrepresented in two of the three negative areas: bilingual classes and EMR classes. As Meier and Stewart have noted, while that pattern does not prove discrimination, it is such a rare pattern that it is very suggestive (Meier and Stewart 1989, 224). We found no differences in the area of student suspensions. Our hypothesized model (see Figure 7.1) predicts that districted electoral systems will have a significant relationship to the number of Mexican American school board members, which in turn will relate to the percentage of Mexican American school administrators. Following the suggested path, the percentage of Mexican American school administrators will relate directly to the percentage of Mexican American teachers. In the area of second-generation discrimination, our hypothe-

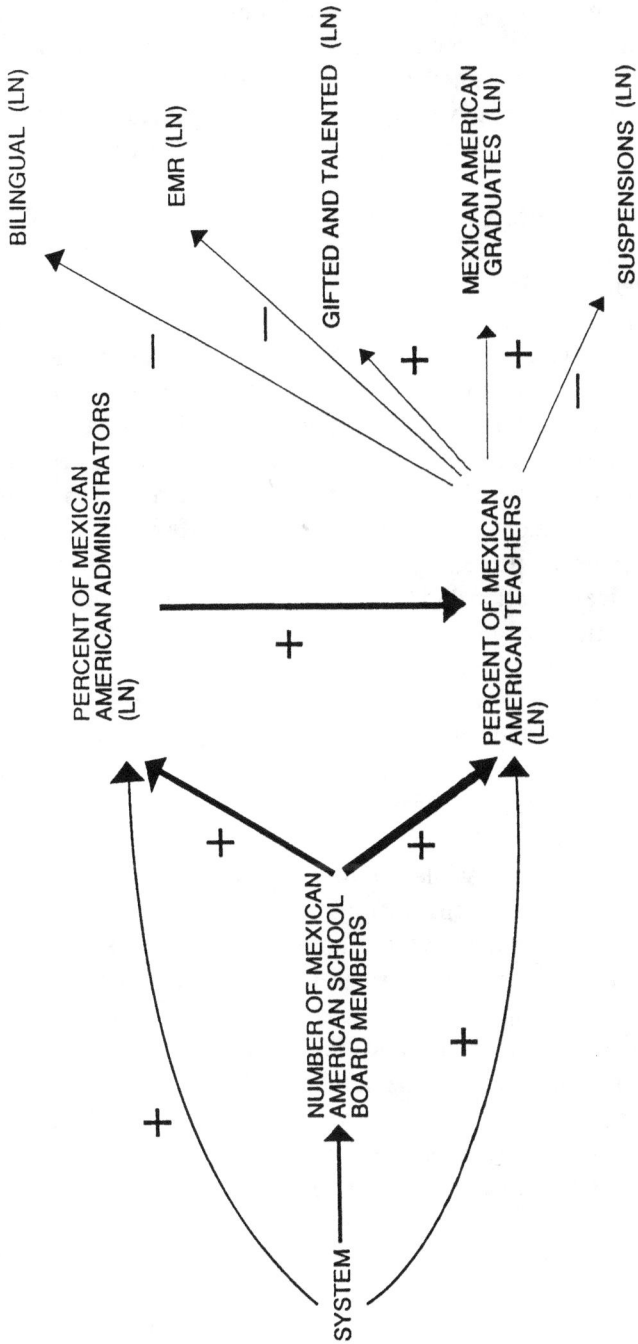

Figure 7.1. **Hypothesized Model of Representational Links to Second-Generation Discrimination**

sized model suggests a direct relationship in a positive direction between Mexican American teachers and the number of Mexican American students assigned to GT programs and the number of Mexican
American students who graduate. The hypothesized model suggests a
direct relationship in a negative direction between the percentage of
Mexican American teachers and the assignment of Mexican American
students to EMR programs and bilingual programs, and between the
percentage of Mexican American teachers and the Mexican American
student graduation rate.

The actual model is presented in Figure 7.2. As anticipated, there
was a statistically significant relationship between the form of electoral
system and the number of Mexican American school board members.
The relationship was in the expected direction—that is, districted systems were related to increased numbers of Mexican American school
board members. The form of electoral system had no statistically significant relationship to the percentage of Mexican American administrators or the percentage of Mexican American teachers. There was a
significant relationship between the form of election system and Mexican American graduation rates, but, curiously, the relationship was
negative; that is, a districted system related directly to depressed graduation rates. It is possible that this relationship reflects a time lag
between the stage at which a school board shifts to districted elections
and the stage at which the effect of that change manifests itself at the
final leg, graduation, of the educational process. This relationship may
also reflect how difficult it is for external factors to affect graduation
rates. It is even possible that the presence of Mexican American school
board members, school administrators, and teachers may have an
ironic affect of encouraging students who might otherwise drop out of
school at a much earlier stage to stay in school through their senior
year, even though their chances of graduation are slim. This would
serve, then, to depress graduation rates.

In the actual model, the number of Mexican American school board
members had a statistically significant effect on both the percentage of
Mexican American administrators and the percentage of Mexican
American teachers. Both relationships were in the anticipated directions: an increase in the number of Mexican American school board
members was related to increases in the percentage of Mexican American administrators and teachers. We also found that the dominant influence on attracting Mexican American teachers was the presence of

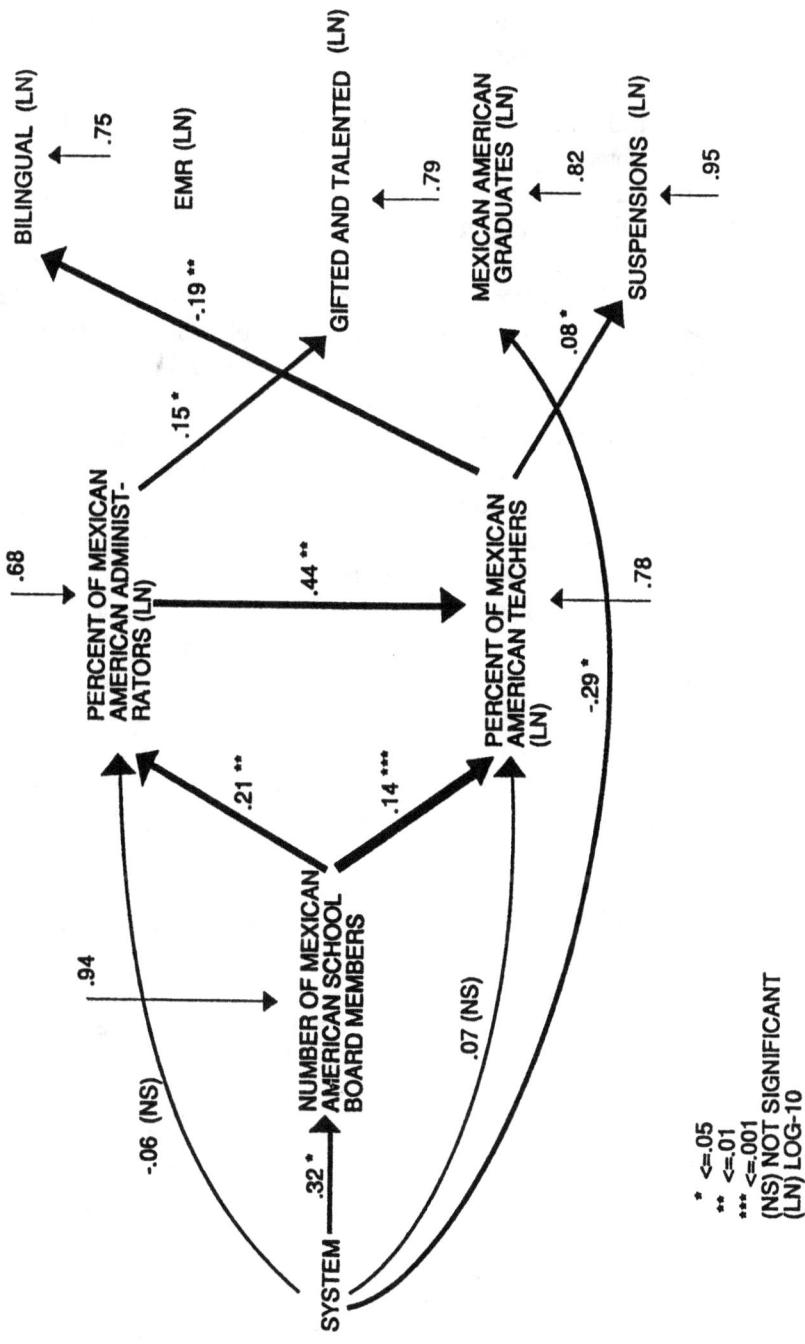

Figure 7.2. Representational Links to Second-Generation Discrimination

SYSTEM

.32 * NUMBER OF MEXICAN AMERICAN SCHOOL BOARD MEMBERS

.94

-.06 (NS)

.21 **

.14 ***

.07 (NS)

PERCENT OF MEXICAN AMERICAN ADMINIST- RATORS (LN)

.68

.44 **

PERCENT OF MEXICAN AMERICAN TEACHERS (LN)

.78

-.29 *

.15 *

-.19 **

.08 *

BILINGUAL (LN)

.75

EMR (LN)

GIFTED AND TALENTED (LN)

.79

MEXICAN AMERICAN GRADUATES (LN)

.82

SUSPENSIONS (LN)

.95

*   <=.05
**   <=.01
***   <=.001
(NS) NOT SIGNIFICANT
(LN) LOG-10

157

Mexican American administrators. In our study, each 1-percentile increase in Mexican American administrators was associated with a 0.44-percentile increase in Mexican American teachers.

While both the number of Mexican American school board members and the percentage of Mexican American administrators directly affected the percentage of Mexican American teachers, we found that the effect of school board members was more influential in the direct linkage than when mediated through percentage of Mexican American administrators. To ascertain this, we multiplied the direct effect between the number of Mexican American school board members and the percentage of Mexican American administrators, and the percentage of Mexican American administrators and the percentage of Mexican American teachers. The strength of the indirect coefficient (0.09) was less in the mediated linkage than the direct effect between the number of Mexican American school board members and the percentage of Mexican American teachers (0.14), but when added to the direct coefficient, a "total" influence of 0.23 resulted.

The actual model suggests four statistically significant relationships with the second-generation discrimination policy areas. As already mentioned, the type of election system had a direct effect on Mexican American graduation rates, although the beta was in an unexpected negative direction. The model also suggests that the percentage of Mexican American administrators had a direct positive relationship with the assignment of Mexican American students to gifted and talented programs.

The percentage of Mexican American teachers had a direct effect on only two of the five second-generation discrimination areas. The relationship between the percentage of Mexican American teachers and the assignment of Mexican American students to bilingual programs was in the expected direction; that is, fewer Mexican American students were assigned to bilingual programs as the percentage of Mexican American teachers increased. However, the effect of the percentage of Mexican American teachers on the Mexican American student suspension rate was in an unexpected positive direction. We expected fewer Mexican American students to be suspended as the percentage of Mexican American faculty increased.

Our analyses indicate that the role teachers play with respect to influencing second-generation discrimination is not as direct as that suggested by the hypothesized model. This finding comports with

Table 7.10

Interactive Term Regressions Dependent Variables:
Mexican American Equity Scores

Independent Variables	Bilingual	Suspen-sions	Gifted	Graduation	EMR
School board x teachers	−0.38**	0.05	0.35**	0.37**	−0.05
Electoral system	−0.16	−0.03	0.09	−0.22	−0.24
Intercept	0.63	−0.02	−0.43	−0.15	0.04
R^2	0.18	0.00	0.14	0.16	0.06
F	6.77	.08	4.78	5.83	2.85
N	21	19	21	21	19

$**p < 0.01$.

Meier and Stewart's suggestion that "effective policy advocacy . . . requires representation both among teachers and on the school board" (1989, 236).

Meier and Stewart used an interactive term to represent the relationship among school board members, teachers, and the second-generation policy areas. We employed the same interactive term to explore that relationship. Table 7.10 reports regressions of the independent variables of form of system and the interactive representational measure. The form of system was coded as 0 = at-large and 1 = single-member districts. The interactive term is a positive percentile expression. We expected these terms to relate directly to the positive policy measures, such as GT and graduation rates. We expected a negative relationship between these two variables and the negative policy measures, such as bilingual assignments, EMR assignments, and suspensions.

We found statistically significant relationships between the interactive variable and the negative policy ratio relating to bilingual equity and the positive policy ratios relating to GT and graduation equity. The R^2 values are as thin; the regression coefficients, however, are in the expected directions: an increase in the interactive term reduced the percentage of Mexican American students assigned to bilingual programs. Here, the R^2 was a modest 0.18. The relationship between the interactive term and the assignment of Mexican American students to GT programs was in the expected direction: the R^3 square was 0.14. We found a positive relationship with the interactive term and the graduation equity score: the R^3 square was 0.16.

No statistically significant relationships between the interactive term and Mexican American suspensions or the assignment of Mexican American students to EMR classes existed. The form of electoral system did not significantly contribute to the equation of any of the policy areas.

Discussion

There is much congruence between the hypothesized model and the actual model. The direct effect of the form of electoral system on the number of Mexican American school board members is no surprise. Previous research suggests that the impact of at-large systems depresses Mexican American representation; consequently, we would expect districted systems to be related to increased numbers of Mexican American school board members.

The positive effect of the number of Mexican American school board members on the percentage of Mexican American administrators supports the national findings of Meier and Stewart (1989, 173–77). This effect comports with findings in other arenas as well; for example, municipal employment of Mexican Americans (Dye and Renick 1981, 483). Meier and Stewart suggest, "The process by which Hispanic administrators are hired is linked to politics in the school district" (1989, 173). Thus, it is not surprising that the election of Mexican Americans to the school boards is linked to an increase in the percentage of Mexican American administrators.

The actual model parallels the hypothesized model's relationship between the percentage of Mexican American administrators and the percentage of Mexican American teachers. A relatively strong coefficient (0.44) in a positive direction suggests a direct relationship between the two variables, a finding consistent with Meier and Stewart (1989, 180, 195). Since school administrators are in charge of hiring teachers for the school district, that relationship was expected.

The actual model also shows a direct relationship between the number of Mexican American school board members and the percentage of Mexican American teachers. Here the beta (0.14) was not as strong as that between the percentage of Mexican American administrators and the percentage of Mexican American teachers, but the relationship is statistically significant. This finding differs from that of Meier and Stewart

(1989, 180), but agrees with an earlier study (Fraga, Meier, and England 1986). Thus, while we agree with Meier and Stewart that the relationship between Mexican American school board members and the percentage of Mexican American teachers is indirectly filtered through increases in the percentage of Mexican American administrators, we also find a direct relationship. This is particularly important when one considers the traditional political role played by school board members in comparison with the professional roles played by administrators and teachers.

In examining the relationships to the second-generation discrimination variables, we found less congruence between the hypothesized model and the empirical model. This was especially so in the relationship of the percentage of Mexican American teachers to the second-generation discrimination variables. Meier and Stewart characterized teachers as "the equivalent of implementation bureaucrats" in a school district (1989, 77). This is so for three reasons. First, teachers may have some discretion in interpreting and administering the school district's policies. Second, previous research suggests that there may be greater empathy between co-ethnic teachers and students (Silver 1973; Smith and June 1982; So 1987). Mexican American teachers likely would be more sensitive to the particular concerns of Mexican American students. Third, and related to the latter point, is the visibility of Mexican American teachers in the capacity of role models for Mexican American students. Because of these factors, we would expect that a higher percentage of Mexican American teachers would attenuate the effects of second-generation discrimination on Mexican American students.

The actual model, however, lends less support to that notion than expected. Of the five policy areas identified as second-generation discrimination, the percentage of Mexican American teachers affected only two in a statistically significant way: the assignment of Mexican American students to bilingual programs and Mexican American student suspension rates. The effect on the assignments to bilingual programs was in the expected direction, with a beta of -0.19. Bilingual programs are often viewed as a subtle form of tracking Mexican American students into classes whose graduation rates are lower than those in the higher-ability tracks. Therefore, a higher percentage of Mexican American teachers should relate to a lower percentage of Mexican American students being assigned to bilingual programs.

The relationship of the percentage of Mexican American teachers to Mexican American student suspension rates is more confusing. Here, as with the assignment to bilingual programs, we expected the percentage of Mexican American teachers to correlate negatively with the suspension rate of Mexican American students. The actual model, however, offered an 0.08 beta in a positive direction. We found no apparent explanation for the anomaly. Although school administrators are the individuals who actually suspend students, teachers play an active role in the suspension process by initiating the referral of the student to the appropriate administrator. Nor did our actual model establish a direct relationship between the percentage of school administrators and the suspension of Mexican American students. The percentage of Mexican American teachers did not have a direct effect on any other second-generation discrimination variables.

The percentage of Mexican American administrators did directly affect the number of Mexican American students assigned to GT programs. The coefficient was 0.15 and statistically significant. At first blush it may seem a bit surprising that there would be a direct relationship here where none is indicated by the actual model between the percentage of Mexican American teachers and the assignments to GT programs. However, while teachers are able to make recommendations concerning assignments to these programs, their recommendations are only part of the assignment process. Parental requests play a very important role, and apparently it often is unwritten policy for administrators to honor parental requests even when such requests override teacher recommendations. School district policies are no less susceptible to such informal political pressures than other institutions in contact with the public.

Meier and Stewart (1991, 109–112) suggested that the effect of Mexican American teachers in general may be a function of interaction with the percentage of Mexican Americans on the school board. Pursuing that suggestion, we modeled this interaction by creating the interactive term and entering it into a regression equation that also included the form of electoral system. Here we found statistically significant relationships between the interactive term and the policy areas of bilingual equity, gifted and talented equity, and graduation equity. The interactive term related positively to gifted and talented equity and graduation equity, but related negatively to bilingual equity. We found no statistically significant relationships between the interactive term and the policy areas of EMR assignments or suspensions; nor did we find a statistically significant relationship between form of electoral system and any of the policy measurements.

Summary

Our data suggest that the model presented at the beginning of this chapter is useful in exploring the impact of district elections on educational policy relating to Mexican American students. A change in electoral structure from at-large to district relates to increases in the number of Mexican American school board members. The number of Mexican American school board members relates to higher percentages of Mexican American school administrators and teachers.

Our data also suggest that the percentage of Mexican Americans on the school boards interacts with the percentage of Mexican American teachers to predict three of the five policy areas we examined.

In brief, then, our data suggest that single-member electoral systems will increase the number of Mexican American school board members, which will increase the number of Mexican American school administrators and teachers. An increase in the number of Mexican American administrators and teachers, in turn, depresses the negative impact of second-generation discrimination ratios. Mexican American students are better served by such districts.

What clearly emerges from these findings is an awareness of how complex the educational process is. One of the more enduring clichés in politics is that "all politics is local." The politics of local education is no exception. The political realities, and the economic realities, of the context in which educational bureaucracies operate serve, we believe, to explain many, if not most, of the different findings produced by our data when compared with those studies that have concentrated only on the larger school districts. That is, the political and economic dynamic in a small school district is sufficiently different from that in a larger district to produce different outcomes.

Notes

1. Our model and use of these measures is derived from Meier, Stewart, and England (1989) and Meier and Stewart (1991). Our discussion and description of these second-generation measures is largely taken from those works. We also thank Ken Meier and Joe Stewart for sharing their data and findings with us.

2. These representational ratios have been criticized by Wainscott and Woodard (1988), who suggest that the use of measures with an unbounded top will skew the results. Essentially, they are raising the problem of outliers. While we acknowledge that outliers may constitute a problem, they can be handled statistically. Stewart and Sheffield's work (1987), as well as that of others, suggests that this poses no significant problem if one utilizes a log transformation of the data. Thus, we take advantage of comparability with previous research and utilize the representational ratios in this research.

As before, we take a natural logarithm of the equity scores (Finn 1982; Tufte 1974).

3. We estimated a number of different equations, utilizing a number of different subsets of the independent variables. The significant equation is the one discussed below.

4. The following analyses are an attempt to replicate many of the findings of Meier and Stewart (1991) for a Mexican American population within a single state. We also use a different form of the path analysis model than that found in chapter 6 of the Meier and Stewart work.

5. We are indebted to Professor Richard Engstrom for his thoughts on this matter.

6. Not only are these results very similar to those of Meier and Stewart (1991), but they are quite consistent with those of Dye and Renick (1981). See Meier and Stewart (1991, 123, n. 26).

8

Summary, Conclusions, and Policy Recommendations

What does all this mean? We have asked whether changing from at-large to district elections has any impact on municipal and educational political processes. We have focused on the impact of districting on two areas: the electoral process and the policy process.

The urban reform movement that took place in the late nineteenth and early twentieth centuries cast a very broad net and was one of the most influential of the many attempts to reform the nature of American politics. A major aim of the reformers was to institute structural reforms that would change not just the structures of government, but also the policies produced by those structures. Put simply, the reformers wanted "better" government. One aim of the proposed reforms was to produce a policy process in which "amateur" elected officials would be guided in their decisions by trained professionals. Ideally, the new council member or school board member would be apolitical, removed from the partisan political machines that characterized political activity during the early part of this century. The reform would lead to policies developed for the good of the whole community, not just some parochial part. And this did, in large part, occur. The urban reform movement produced a city council that had a distinctly apolitical, upper-middle-class bias. However, yesterday's reforms are tomorrow's problems and, less than a century after the beginnings of the urban reform movement, another major American reform began: the Civil Rights movement. This reform movement, with its concern for equal treatment of minorities, also saw political structure as a key to change. With the passage of the Voting Rights Act in 1965, the stage was set for the use of litigation as a tool to effect structural change that benefits minorities. Probably the most common change has been the return to district or ward elections. Prodded for the most part by such organized groups as MALDEF and Southwest Voter Registration and Education Project, and prodded in part as well by what one city manager described as simply "being the right thing to do," for the past two decades cities and school districts have adopted a variety of districting schemes aimed at enhancing minority representation. We have addressed two important questions concerning these moves toward districting. First, did the change to districts enhance minority representation? And, second, what was the policy impact of such change on the minority communities?

In response to the first question, our data support the conventional wisdom of earlier research: changing to districts increases the number of Mexican Americans seeking council and school board seats. We also found that, not only did more Mexican Americans run, but also more Mexican Americans won. In terms of representational equity— that is, the percentage of Mexican Americans on a city council or a school board compared with the Mexican American population percentage—we found a general rise in the equity scores during the postdistricting period. Another change noted in the postdistricted electoral arena was an increase in the number of Mexican American candidates who ran and won while residing in Mexican American neighborhoods. Prior to districting the city councils, for example, it was more common for Mexican American council members from the various cities to live in predominantly Anglo residential areas; that pattern changed following districting.

City Councils

Our data show that there are significant differences between officials elected by district and those elected at-large. There are also significant differences between Mexican American council members and Anglo council members. District elections tend to result in council members with a decidedly neighborhood orientation. Once elected, it is clear that the ethnic and district council members adopt a different representational style. They tend to devote more time and attention than their at-large counterparts on city business, and more time performing constituent services. This is not to say that the Mexican American council members are only "errand boys." However, these members have a constituency service orientation quite distinct from that of the at-large council members and the Anglo council members. This representational and constituency focus distinction may help explain the development of voting blocs and reported increases in conflict among council members after the change to a district form of election.

While council members in general are well educated, moderate conservative males, Mexican American council members tend to be somewhat younger, less well educated, and more conservative than their Anglo counterparts. They also are more likely than Anglos to view the city council as a stepping-stone to higher political office. We believe the latter point is particularly important. City council elections may serve as the first step on the path to higher political office for Mexican American public officials. City council campaigns will provide valuable experience and a constituent base for later campaigns, both of which previously had been denied to this particular group. There is likely, in other words, to be a "ripple" effect caused by districting at the city council level, as over the years Mexican American councilpersons use their initial elections as a booster for higher office.

Our second question focuses on whether the election of increased numbers of Mexican Americans translated into policy changes. This question goes beyond the symbolic gains of electoral victories. The first indication of a change in what a districted council does is reflected in procedure rather than substance. We believe that the election of Mexican American council members, often for the first time in the community's history, frequently alters the dynamics of council behavior. Heilig and Mundt (1984) write of minorities having a "voice at city hall." Parker (1990, 164–65) writes of the symbolic value to blacks of having black city council members serve. Even though the minority voice might be a lone one, representation can be both symbolic and substantive. One vote might not be able to carry council decisions. However, the minority councilperson can represent his or her neighborhood very well. Virtually all of the city managers we interviewed report that, following districting, more council policies are made in a distributive fashion so all parts of the city benefit. As one city manager said, "If I pave streets on the North [Anglo] side of town, I pave streets on the South [Mexican American] side." Our research also indicates that minority council members often serve as an "expanded" form of representative. Many times co-ethnics seek out the ethnic councilperson even when he or she does not represent their district. Thus, not only do the ethnic constituents of the district that the Mexican American council member represents have a voice, but Mexican Americans residing in other districts also view the Mexican American council member as "their" representative.

Still, does it make any substantive policy difference to the Mexican American community if district elections replace at-large elections? Our data support the conclusion that substantial differences occur not only in the electoral arena but also in the policy arena.

We find that under district systems, the presence of Mexican Americans on the city council influences the policy decisions of the council in the areas of municipal employment, municipal salaries, and the appointment of Mexican Americans to city boards and commissions. Following districting, more Mexican Americans are hired in the higher ranks of municipal employees and relatively fewer are employed at the very lowest levels. Further, more Mexican Americans are employed at the middle and upper pay levels of the cities; in some cities the change is quite dramatic. Finally, more Mexican Americans are appointed to the important municipal boards and commissions, providing an important "training ground" for new Mexican American representatives.

Recently, Meier and Smith found that "As a bureaucracy becomes more representative so does political representation" (1993, 13). This indicates that increases in minority representation in the bureaucracy also effect increases in minority political representation. Cities with expanded Mexican American representation at the middle and upper levels of the bureaucracy are quite likely to be different cities from those without such bureaucratic representation.

School Boards

Our data concerning school boards in Texas follow a pattern similar to the city council data. The data indicate that there are significant differences based on ethnicity and election structure between board members. Anglo board members are more likely to have higher incomes and higher levels of education; they also are more likely to be conservative and to have a longer term of service on the school board. Mexican American board members are more likely to have lived longer in the community than their Anglo counterparts. Mexican American board members are more likely than Anglos to seek office for the purpose of serving their neighborhoods and in response to a concern over a particular issue. In short, substantial differences exist.

In terms of electoral structure, Mexican Americans are more likely than Anglos to be elected from districts, and district board members tend to have lived in the community longer and to have served on the school board for less time than at-large members. District board members are more likely than those elected at-large to seek office for the purpose of serving their neighborhoods and for the purpose of reacting to a single issue. Having a school district change from an at-large to a district system is viewed by the courts as a remedy for past discrimination against Mexican Americans. Given our findings reported above, it seems safe to suggest that, as the number of minorities on school boards increases, a change in the role identification and behavior of school board members will also occur. School districts that have minority members tend to perform differently from districts without minority members. So we ask again, as we did with the city councils: Do the electoral changes among school board representation resulting from districting translate into policy changes for the minority community?

We have noted earlier Tucker and Zeigler's (1977, 11) argument that school boards are inefficient vehicles for citizens to influence educational policy. Our demonstration of significant differences between school board members, both demographically and in terms of representational foci, based on ethnicity and electoral form, lead us to suggest that this is not necessarily the case, especially for minority populations. The enhanced levels of conflict on school boards after districting, and the linkage of higher levels of conflict with constituency interests validate this suggestion. School boards with more minority and constituency-oriented members, both of which result from districting, can influence educational policy.

A change in electoral structure from at-large to district increases the number of Mexican American school board members. The number of Mexican American school board members relates to higher percentages of Mexican American school administrators and teachers. Thus, form of election increases not only Mexican American political representation, but also Mexican American bureaucratic representation. An increase in the number of Mexican American administrators has a strong positive effect on the number of Mexican American "street-level bureaucrats" in the educational system: teachers.

Our data suggest that district electoral systems will increase the number of Mexican American school board members, which will increase the number of Mexican American school administrators and teachers. An increase in the number of Mexican American administrators and teachers, in turn, depresses the negative impact of second-generation discrimination ratios. Specifically, expanded Mexican American political and bureaucratic representation influences the assignment of Mexican American students to bilingual classes, and assignment to gifted and talented classes. In addition, such representation influences the suspension rate of Mexican American students. We believe that these findings indicate that Mexican American students are better served by such districts.

Council Members and School Board Members Compared

Comparing the responses to our survey from city council members with the responses from school board members, we find many similarities. Perhaps this is not surprising; both entities are important policy-making bodies at the local level. Mexican American council members and school board members are less well educated than Anglos and tend to have lived in their communities longer than Anglos, probably reflecting a less mobile group with strong community attachments. Mexican American elected officials are more likely than Anglos to view running for office as a way of increasing business contacts. This may well indicate that ethnic officials may be viewed as upwardly mobile. At the same time we find some intra-ethnic differences between Mexican American council members and Mexican American school board members. Although both Mexican American council members and school board members are more likely to be conservative than liberal (as are Anglos), Mexican American school board members are much less conservative than their city council counterparts. In addition, we found that Mexican American council members are more likely than Mexican American school board members to view their current elected positions as stepping-stones to higher office. This relative lack of political ambition on the part of ethnic school board members supports the notion of school board members as less political than co-ethnics serving in other forms of governance.

Other Findings

Our findings suggest that the structure and representation literature can be fully integrated into urban research and theory. Research on urban minority representation and policy can be reconciled with Peterson's assertion that local governments are inherently limited in what they can do to satisfy local demands (1981). While some urban scholars might reject the view of cities (and by implication, school districts) as "independent policy producing units," where local government officials have a considerable amount of substantive policy-making discretion (see Peterson 1981), we do not. We believe that cities and school districts can affect their own well-being.

Election structure and minority representation are directly linked to regime theory (Stone 1989) and incorporation theory (Browning, Marshall, and Tabb 1984). There is a considerable conceptual overlap between Browning, Marshall, and Tabb's political incorporation concept, Stone's regime politics concept, and the role of election structures for minority representation. Browning, Marshall, and Tabb (1984) argue that political incorporation leads to substantive policy consequences. The level of political incorporation increases when minority council members are elected. Our findings concerning minority representation in Texas cities and school boards support that position. Expanded Mexican American representation often leads to increased political incorporation. The presence of minority council members generally alters the intracouncil dynamics. Often a result of such an alteration is the development of distributive policies that are universalistic, so as to "incorporate" the minority council member into the dominant coalition on the council. Council conflict often increases immediately after the shift to district elections, but then recedes to a more normal level.

Our findings also support the linkage between electoral change, minority representation, and regime change. Minority council members are not elected in a vacuum. Their election often is the result of a combination of increased opportunity due to districts and the enhancement or creation of new coalitions supporting their electoral attempts. In many cases, the minority council member had to create a coalition for support. After the change to district elections, the increased neighborhood focus often spawns new neighborhood advocacy groups that pressure city hall. In addition, it is interesting that our data show that a higher percentage of council members elected by district, rather than at-large, report that support by business groups was important to their election.

Policy Recommendations

Electoral Reform

If the goal is to enhance minority political representation, clearly district elections are an appropriate remedy to minority vote dilution. It does not follow that district elections should be the *sole* remedy; indeed, where there is minority population dispersion, district elections may not be desirable. But it is likely that district elections will remain the traditional remedy to enhance minority representation for much of this decade.[1]

The bulk of the scholarship, buttressed by research findings by expert witnesses for cities, supports districting as a remedy. As our findings indicate, districting is particularly potent in those cities with significant and identifiable levels of residential segregation, and where the community is less than 55 percent Mexican American. In such cases district elections would seem to be an appropriate remedy, and we continue to urge their adoption as a means to electoral equity.

As we observed above, however, there are situations in which districting may not be an appropriate remedy. This is most often so where the minority community is residentially dispersed, making it difficult to draw "compact, contiguous" electoral districts in which minorities would have a substantial chance of winning. This is even more so now that the U.S. Supreme Court has indicated it will not treat eccentric racial gerrymandering casually. Although it will be some time before the effects of *Shaw* v. *Reno* are fully known, the decision surely gives pause to those who heretofore drew districts with little thought as to geographical integrity.

There are other remedies available that will encourage minority electoral empowerment, and we suggest it is important that no community or school district ignore them. Perhaps the most popular alternative is cumulative voting. As Cole and Taebel put it,

> Because its effectiveness is not dependent on a high degree of residential segregation, cumulative voting is particularly appropriate for those

situations where minorities are fairly evenly dispersed throughout the community. Using the cumulative vote procedure, each voter is allocated a number of votes equal to the number of seats to be filled at any particular election. Voters may aggregate or cumulate their votes and cast them in any combination of preferences. If there are five seats to be filled in a particular election, as an example, voters may cast all five votes for one candidate, or they may spread their votes among as many as five candidates in any combination. (1992, 195)

While there is not extensive experience with cumulative voting in the United States, we do have some information about its effectiveness. Cole and his colleagues have extensively studied the Alamogordo, New Mexico, experience with cumulative voting (Cole and Taebel 1992; Cole, Taebel, and Engstrom 1990; Engstrom, Taebel, and Cole 1989). They have found (1992, 200) that cumulative voting does enhance minority electoral success. They conclude that it is a viable alternative to single-member districts in the cases of residentially dispersed minorities.

Several years prior to Cole and Taebel's scholarship, a legal note in the *Yale Law Journal* also sang the praises of cumulative voting (Note 1982, 144–60). Criticizing the use of single-member districts because of "collateral effects," such as an increase in residential segregation and a reinforcement of "race consciousness" (1982, 147), the article explored the use of three alternative remedies: cumulative voting, the single transferable vote, and limited voting. Although the latter two were preferable to single-member districts, both suffered weaknesses not found in cumulative voting. Consequently, cumulative voting was urged as the appropriate remedy for minority vote dilution (1982, 153–59).

Cumulative voting, however, is not well understood and is not widely used, so there probably will be initial resistance. In at least one of our research cities, the possibility of cumulative voting was raised by the attorney for the plaintiff in discussions with the city, but was not pursued by the city. In that case, the ability to draw districts allowed the minority plaintiffs to achieve their goal.

One obstacle to the adoption of cumulative voting may be the firm establishment in judicial precedent of districting as the appropriate remedy to voting rights litigation. Courts generally treat precedent with respect, so the election of alternative remedies is likely to be characterized by a very deliberate process.

However, in those cases where it is appropriate, those persons seeking enhanced minority empowerment would be well served to explore the use of cumulative voting, as well as other potential reforms.[2]

Other Electoral Reforms

If the goal is to achieve electoral equity, both plaintiffs and defendants in voting rights litigation may want to consider increasing the size of the city council. Research has shown that minorities are advantaged by larger governing bodies (Bullock and MacManus 1993; Taebel 1978). In addition, larger councils offer greater opportunity to empower different minority communities. However, one of the consequences of larger councils may be increased conflict and a more difficult managerial role for city managers. Obviously, city managers can play a vital role in the empowerment of minorities. The larger council size and attendant increase in conflict offer an opportunity for city managers to serve as mediators, and allow for more political incorporation for Mexican American councilpersons.

Our data show that one outcome of enhanced Mexican American representation on Texas city councils has been the increase in Mexican American employment at middle to upper levels of city bureaucracies, along with an increase in pay equity for Mexican Americans in municipal employment. We suggest that minorities aim not only at electoral victory, not only at achieving a "voice at City Hall," but focus efforts at municipal reform in these two areas as well. The interesting finding by Meier and Smith (1993) that enhanced bureaucratic representation of minorities can lead to enhanced political representation suggests that this goal can have substantial impact in more than one sense. Thus, we suggest that minorities pursue not only an electoral strategy but also a bureaucratic employment strategy. These are not, of course, mutually exclusive.

Another problem that has emerged in the 1990s is the conflict that may exist between two or more racial or language minorities. The Voting Rights Act did not anticipate this problem, and districts as a remedy may not be appropriate. The recent redistricting of the New York City Council is an example. Macchiarola and Diaz (1993) report the difficulties encountered when trying to apply the restrictions of the VRA to the multiethnic needs of the Manhattan community. They call for vision beyond the VRA to address the growing needs to satisfy an increasingly diverse polity (1993, 57).

School Reforms

We endorse a revitalization of the role of school boards in the American political system. The current system denies the true political role of elected school boards. In fact, Zeigler and his colleagues (Zeigler, Kehoe, and Reisman 1985, 87) speak of the schizophrenic nature of educational governance in this country. We agree. The operative question, it seems to us, is not whether to revitalize the American school board, but how best to achieve the desired results. One way to truly involve the public in the process is to use the public as a source of ideas and guidance, rather than as a source of building support for pet projects of the superintendent. Lyke (1968) argues that the lack of political representation and lack of diversity among school board members make it difficult for citizens to ask questions and for school board members to legitimize controversial decisions. Zeigler, Kehoe, and Reisman (1985, 168) suggest that if educational professionals allowed for greater public participation, public support for schools might be increased.

Another means of enhancing the impact of school boards is to change the electoral nature of school district elections. There is a need to move away from a "politics of low visibility." The current system tends to favor low-turnout elections. The general literature on voting in school board elections amply supports the low turnout (Minar 1966; Sande 1983; Taebel 1977). Iannaccone and Lutz (1970, 22) argue that voter turnout in education board elections is related to organized efforts to turn out the vote of a particular group and to the saliency of issues in any given election. The insulation of educational politics from the political mainstream by means of nonpartisan elections and differential timing (most school board elections are held in the spring) virtually guarantees a low turnout and thus less influence for the board, except in times of crisis. Sande (1983) found that school board elections that were held on the same day as general elections had a much higher rate of turnout than those elections in "reformed" systems. We suggest that the timing of the elections be changed, moving them back to the fall and holding them in concert with other state and local elections.

We also suggest that school boards be increased in size from the average of seven that now exists. This suggestion follows our earlier suggestion to enlarge the size of the city councils. Larger school boards can make it possible for more (and different) minority interests to be represented. If additional available school board seats allow the representation of cohesive neighborhoods, the school board will have the capacity, and the political necessity, to respond to interests expressed by those neighborhoods.

Another avenue that might be explored by those interested in minority political empowerment is the re-creation of the Mexican American School Board Association or some similar organization. Our research joins others (Lujan 1976) in finding different representational interests for Mexican American board members. The Mexican American School Board Association existed in Texas for a brief period in the early 1970s and served not only as a training vehicle for Mexican American school board members, but also as a lobby group representing Mexican American educational interests before state commissions. The current increase in Mexican American school board members statewide would seem to indicate that a sufficient clientele exists. Such an association could serve not only as a source of training for newly elected Mexican American school board members, but also as an important recruitment and mobilizing force for the Mexican American community.

The educational reform movement toward decentralizing power in school districts has led some reformers to postulate a different role for school boards. Strike argues that school boards should act, not as a policy-making body for educational policies, but as a "sovereign of last resort" (1993, 268). Strike sees the board acting only when the interests of the community as a whole are substantially at stake. In other cases, the individual schools, apparently guided by the educational professionals, would have substantial autonomy. This, of course, comes very close to the idea of Chubb and Moe about choice in school systems. Implicit in this argument is the idea that large bureaucracies act so as to reduce educational performance (Smith and Meier 1993). The recent work of Smith and Meier (1993) disputes this claim, and we suggest that this is not the appropriate role for school boards. Instead, school boards should act to hire administrators and teachers, especially minority administrators and teachers, and then assist them in the pursuance of policy goals set with input from the community.

Final Thoughts

As political scientists, we take some comfort in quantitative data, which offer bases of comparison not just between cities but between studies as well. There is a certain "security" to such data; they are "tangible" and offer at least visible, if not statistically significant, bases on which to draw conclusions and inferences.

The most significant impacts of districting, however, may well elude quantification. The link between the representative and the represented does not lend itself to measurement, even in this day of sophisticated survey research. We talk about representational roles and of delegates, trustees, and politicos, but we cannot establish with scientific certainty the nature of identification between a representative and his or her constituency.

It is clear, however, from our interviews with city managers that important changes have occurred in the representational role of the council members. Over and over again we were told that the newly elected Mexican American council members viewed their role on the council as one of directly representing the Mexican American community, to be an "advocate" for "their people". General policy decisions, especially those affecting budget allocations and municipal services, were described by various managers as a function of bargaining and coalition building between council members representing their districts. The thrust of virtually all the city managers, both those who preferred districting and those who preferred at-large systems, was that districting was a more representative system because the Mexican American community had a direct link to the council where none had existed before. We have no reason to doubt that similar changes occur when school board members are elected by districts.

This impact is impossible to quantify, yet it may be the most significant impact of all. For how does one evaluate the effect or "feel" of believing, perhaps for the first time, that one is represented in the councils of government, that one actually has a voice, and consequently, a stake in the political process?

It is not easy to place these changes in perspective. Karnig and Welch (1980) note that several factors may be particularly salient in restricting the impact that increased minority representation has on municipal policy processes. Among the most important of these factors is the passage of time. Several of the cities and school boards examined in our study have only recently changed their election systems. If Karnig and Welch are correct—and we believe they are—the impacts and changes we have noted are incomplete.

The basic nature of American policy making is rooted in incrementalism. In the "Mother, may I?" game of the American policy process, there are not very many "giant" steps, but rather a continuing series of "baby" steps. It is likely that policy changes as a result of increased minority representation will reflect this incremental nature. Academic research undertaken close in time to the period of change must, of necessity, be tentative. Again, we echo Karnig and Welch and encourage the observation of these policy processes over time.

So we end where we began, acknowledging the continuing experiment of the democratic process. We are a generation removed from the initial enactment of the VRA, and it is clear that its impact on our representational system is not yet concluded. For all of our inquiry into electoral equity, employment equity, and pay equity, what we really are about is trying to understand this nebulous notion of self-government. We repeat what one city manager said: "Perhaps the [Mexican American] community believes they are better represented [under the new districting system], but I've noticed no other changes."

Then, he paused and somewhat sheepishly said, "Of course, that's an important change."

Indeed it is.

Notes

1. One of the leading experts in this area, Bernard Grofman, suggests that this might well be the case and that school districts will follow the lead of cities in the adoption of districts (Grofman 1993a).

2. Still (1984, 1992) has analyzed the use of reform measures other than cumulative voting and suggests (1992, 191) that limited voting, in addition to cumulative voting, has a positive effect on black representation.

Appendix A: Survey Questionnaire— Elected City/Town Council Members

Please Answer the following questions about your community and its governing body:

1. What is the size of your town or city?
   a. ( ) Less than 5,000
   b. ( ) 5,001 - 10,000
   c. ( ) 10,001 - 25,000
   d. ( ) 25,000 - 50,000
   e. ( ) 50,001 - 100,000
   f. ( ) 100,001 - 250,000
   g. ( ) 250,001 - 500,000
   h. ( ) Over 500,000

2. How many members (including the mayor) are on the town/city council? _____

3. What type of election system is used in your community?
   ( ) At large (Go to question 4)
   ( ) District (Go to question 3b)
   ( ) Mixed (Go to question 3a)

   3a. If mixed, from which form are you elected?
   ( ) At large (Go to question 3c)
   ( ) District (Go to question 3b)

   3b. If elected from a district, is your district predominately:
   ( ) White/Anglo   ( ) Mexican American
   ( ) Black   ( ) Mixed

   3c. In what year did your city/town switch from at large elections to either district or mixed elections? Year_____

4. In general, would you say there are blocs or factions on the council that persist in voting as a group on a number of issues?
   ( ) NO, there are no real factions on the council.
   ( ) YES, there are some factions on the council, but they are not very strong.
   ( ) YES, there are sharp factions on the council.

5. In your judgment, what percentage of council decisions which you consider important are made unanimously or near unanimously?
   ( ) Over 75%,   ( ) 50-75%,
   ( ) 25-49%,   ( ) Less than 25%

6. In recent years, would you say that conflict on the council has:
   ( ) Increased, ( ) Decreased, ( ) Stayed the Same.

   6a. If your city/town changed its form of election to a district or mixed system within the last few years, has the conflict increased, decreased or stayed about the same since the change to district/mixed?
   ( ) Increased, ( ) Decreased, ( ) Stayed the Same.

7. How many years (including the current one) have you served on the council?
   Circle One: 1 2 3 4 5 6 7 8 9 10 11 12 13+

8. Do you schedule any type of regular gathering to meet with your constituents, and if so, how often?
   ( ) I schedule no such regular meetings.
   ( ) I schedule one or more such meetings a month
   ( ) I schedule regular meetings, but less than 1 a month

9. Approximately how many hours a week do you devote to your job as a member of the city council? _____Hours

   9a. Of the total number of hours per week, how many do you spend doing services for people? _____Hours

10. On the whole, would you say that voters are more interested in your taking care of their personal needs for them or are they more interested in your stands on issues before the council?
    ( ) They are primarily concerned with my issue positions
    ( ) Constituent service and issue positions are about equally important.
    ( ) They are primarily concerned with servicing their needs.

11. Some people view politics in terms of liberals v. conservatives. How would you describe yourself on a liberal-conservative dimension?
    a. ( ) Very Conservative
    b. ( ) Conservative
    c. ( ) Slightly Conservative
    d. ( ) Middle of the Road
    e. ( ) Slightly Liberal
    f. ( ) Liberal
    g. ( ) Very Liberal

12. We would like to know why you initially decided to seek election to the city/town. Please rate the importance of each of the following factors in influencing your decision to run for a council seat. Circle best response.

Very Important	Somewhat Important	Not Very Important	
X	X	X	A. Because I was persuaded by a political party organization.
X	X	X	B. To serve my neighborhood.
X	X	X	C. As a stepping stone to some other political office.
X	X	X	D. To serve the district as a whole.
X	X	X	E. To increase business contacts.
X	X	X	F. Because I enjoy politics and I was looking for a worthwhile activity
X	X	X	G. Because of a strong concern I had about some specific issue. Please identify the issue(s)

13. Please express your agreement or disagreement with each of the following statements on the following scale. Circle one.   (1)=Strongly Agree (2)=Agree (3)=Neutral (4)=Disagree (5)=Strongly Disagree

1 2 3 4 5   I would prefer to raise taxes rather than cut back on city services.

1 2 3 4 5   It is important to have a city plan that shapes the future development of our city.

1 2 3 4 5   Unionization of city employees seriously damages the ability of our elected leaders.

1 2 3 4 5   Generally, I approve of unlimited development in this city; if business wants to invest in new housing or new businesses, the city should go along.

1 2 3 4 5   Our city's resources should be distributed on the basis of need--even if this means some parts of the city will get more than others.

1 2 3 4 5   Federal aid to cities should be increased.

1 2 3 4 5   I believe we should generate new city revenue through user charges rather than through new taxes or tax increases.

14. Prior to running for the city council were you active in other local/state/national campaigns--that is, were you politically active?
( ) NO (Go to question 15)
( ) YES

14a. If you were active, how many campaigns were you active in? (Circle one) 1, 2, 3, 4, 5 or more.

15. Council member's represent many different constituencies. In your own view, how important is your representation of each of the following constituencies? Circle your response.

Very Important	Somewhat Important	Not Very Important	
X	X	X	A. A geographic area of the city or a neighborhood.
X	X	X	B. A racial or ethnic group
X	X	X	C. A partisan or ideological constituency such as Democrat or Republican.
X	X	X	D. The city/town as a whole.
X	X	X	E. A single issue group such as abortion, tax-cutting, government reform, etc.
X	X	X	F. A business constituency.
X	X	X	G. A labor union or public employee constituency.

16. How is the mayor of your city elected?
( ) Independent election
( ) From the Council

17. How important were each of the following in your last campaign in terms of giving money, helping in your campaign in some way, or providing other kinds of support.

Very Important	Somewhat Important	Not Very Important	
X	X	X	A. Your political party
X	X	X	B. Organized labor
X	X	X	C. Business groups or leaders
X	X	X	D. Neighborhood organizations
X	X	X	E. Organized racial or ethnic groups.
X	X	X	F. Groups organized over a single issue (Please specify)

_____

Finally, we would like to know something about your background. Remember that all answers are strictly confidential and will only be used for statistical analysis.

18. Gender   ( ) Male.   ( ) Female

19. Race/Ethnicity.   ( ) Hispanic
( ) Black
( ) White
( ) Other

20. In what year were you born? _____

21. How many years have you lived in your present community? _____ years.

22. What is/was your usual occupation prior to running for the city council? _____

23. What is the highest level of formal education you have completed?
( ) High School or less
( ) Some college
( ) College graduate
( ) Professional or graduate school

24. Which of the following categories best reflects your gross family income in 1991? Check one.
( ) Less than $15,000
( ) $15,000 - $24,999
( ) $25,000 - $34,999
( ) $35,000 - $44,999
( ) $45,000 - $54,999
( ) $55,000 - $64,999
( ) $65,000 - $74,999
( ) $75,000 and above

Thank you for completing the questionnaire. Please return in the enclosed envelope to the Social Science Department, Univ. of Texas, Brownsville, Tx. 78520

Appendix B: Survey Questionnaire— Elected School Board Members

First, we would like to know something about your community and its governing body:

1. What is the size of your town or city?
( ) Less than 5,000   ( ) 50,001 - 100,000
( ) 5,001 - 10,000   ( ) 100,001 - 250,000
( ) 10,001 - 25,000   ( ) 250,001 - 500,000
( ) 25,000 - 50,000   ( ) Over 500,000

2. How many members are on the district school board? _____

3. What type of election system is used in your school district?
( ) At large   (Go to question 4)
( ) District   (Go to question 3b)
( ) Mixed   (Go to question 3a)

3a. If mixed, from which form are you elected?
( ) At large   (Go to question 3c)
( ) District   (Go to question 3b)

3b. If elected from a district, is your district predominately:
( ) White/Anglo   ( ) Mexican American
( ) Black   ( ) Mixed

3c. In what year did your school district switch from at large elections to either district or mixed elections? Year_____

4. In general, would you say there are blocs or factions on the board that persist in voting as a group on a number of issues?
( ) NO, there are no real cleavages on the board.
( ) YES, there are some cleavages on the board but they are not very strong.
( ) YES, there are sharp cleavages on the board.

5. In your judgment, what percentage of board decisions which you consider important are made unanimously or near unanimously?
( ) Over 75%,   ( ) 50-75%,
( ) 25-49%,   ( ) Less than 25%

6. In recent years, would you say that conflict on the board has:
( ) Increased, ( ) Decreased, ( ) Stayed the Same.

6a. If your school district changed its form of election to a district or mixed system within the last few years, has the conflict increased, decreased or stayed about the same since the change to district/mixed?
( ) Increased, ( ) Decreased, ( ) Stayed the Same.

7. How many years (including the current one) have you served on the board?
Circle One: 1 2 3 4 5 6 7 8 9 10 11 12 13+

8. Approximately how may hours a week do you devote to your job as a member of the school district board?
_____Number of hours.

8a. Of the total number of hours per week, how many do you spend doing services for people?
_____Number of hours

9. On the whole, would you say that voters are more interested in your taking care of their personal needs for them or are they more interested in your stands on issues before the board?
( )They are primarily concerned with my issue positions.
( ) Constituent service and issue positions are about equally important.
( ) They are primarily concerned with servicing their needs.

10. Some people view politics in terms of liberals v. conservatives. How would you describe yourself on a liberal-conservative dimension?
a. ( ) Very Conservative   e. ( ) Slightly Liberal
b. ( ) Conservative   f. ( ) Liberal
c. ( ) Slightly Conservative g. ( ) Very Liberal
d. ( ) Middle of the Road

11. We would like to know why you initially decided to seek election to the school board. Please rate the importance of each of the following factors in influencing your decision to run for the school board seat. Circle response.

Very Important	Somewhat Important	Not Very Important	
X	X	X	A. Because I was persuaded by a political party organization.
X	X	X	B. To serve my neighborhood.
X	X	X	C. As a stepping stone to some other political office.
X	X	X	D. To serve the district as a whole.
X	X	X	E. To increase business contacts.
X	X	X	F. Because I enjoy politics and I was looking for a worthwhile activity
X	X	X	G. Because of a strong concern I had about some specific issue. Please identify the issue(s) _____

12. Please express your agreement or disagreement with each of the following statements using the following scale: (1)=Strongly Agree (2)=Agree (3)=Neutral (4)=Disagree (5)=Strongly Disagree. Circle response.

1 2 3 4 5   I would prefer to raise taxes rather than cut back on school district services.

1 2 3 4 5   Unionization of school district employees seriously damages the ability of our elected leaders.

1 2 3 4 5   Generally, I approve of unlimited development in this school district; if business wants to invest in new housing or new businesses, the school district should go along.

1 2 3 4 5   Our school district's resources should be distributed on the basis of need--even if this means some parts of the school deistrict will get more than others.

1 2 3 4 5   Drug education should be given greater emphasis in schools.

1 2 3 4 5   Family planning should be given greater emphasis in schools.

13. Prior to running for the school district board were you active in other local/state/national campaigns--that is, were you politically active?
( ) NO (Go to question 14)
( ) YES

13a. If you were active, how many campaigns were you active in? (Circle one) 1 2 3 4 5 or more.

14. Board member's may represent different constituencies. In your own view, how important is your representation of each of the following constituencies? Circle your response.

Very Important	Somewhat Important	Not Very Important	
X	X	X	A. A geographic area of the city or a neighborhood.
X	X	X	B. A racial or ethnic group
X	X	X	C. A partisan or ideological constituency such as Democrat or Republican.
X	X	X	D. The district as a whole.
X	X	X	E. A single issue group such as abortion, tax-cutting, government reform, etc.
X	X	X	F. A business constituency.
X	X	X	G. A labor union or public employee constituency.

15. As an elected official, what issue or issues do you see as being the most important facing your school district in the next few years?

_____
_____
_____

Finally, we would like to know something about your background. Remember that all answers are strictly confidential and will only be used for statistical analysis.

16. Gender   ( ) Male.   ( ) Female

17. Race/Ethnicity. ( ) Latino
( ) Black
( ) White
( ) Other

18. In what year were you born? _____

19. How many years have you lived in your present community? _____years.

20. What is/was your usual occupation prior to running for the school district board? _____

21. What is the highest level of formal education you have completed?
( ) High School or less
( ) Some college
( ) College graduate
( ) Professional or graduate school

22. Which of the following categories best reflects your gross family income in 1991? Check one.
( ) Less than $15,000
( ) $15,000 - $24,999
( ) $25,000 - $34,999
( ) $35,000 - $44,999
( ) $45,000 - $54,999
( ) $55,000 - $64,999
( ) $65,000 - $74,999
( ) $75,000 and above

Thank you for completing the questionnaire. Please return in the enclosed envelope to the Social Science Department, 80 Ft. Brown, University of Texas, Brownsville, Texas 78520

References

Abrams, Kathryn. 1988. "Raising Politics Up: Minority Political Participation and Section 2 of the Voting Rights Act." *New York University Law Review 63* (June): 449–531.

Acuna, Rodolfo. 1981. *Occupied America: A History of Chicanos*, 2d ed. New York: Harper and Row.

———. 1981. *Occupied America: A History of Chicanos*, 3d ed. New York: Harper and Row.

Agresti, Alan. 1984. *Analysis of Ordinal Categorical Data*. New York: Wiley.

Aldrich, John H., and Nelson, Forrest D. 1984. *Linear Probability, Logit and Probit Models*. Newbury Park, CA: Sage.

Allsup, Carl. 1977. "Education Is Our Freedom: The American G.I. Forum and the Mexican American School Segregation in Texas, 1948–1957." *Aztlan 8*: 27–49.

Allsup, Vernon Carl. 1976. *The American GI Forum: A History of a Mexican-American Organization*. Unpublished Ph.D. dissertation, University of Texas at Austin.

———. 1982. *The American G.I. Forum: Origins and Evolution*. Austin: Center for Mexican American Studies, University of Texas Press.

Alvarez, Rodolfo. 1973. "The Psycho-Historical and Socioeconomic Development of the Chicano Community in the United States." *Social Science Quarterly 53*: 920–42.

Anders, Evan. 1982. *Boss Rule in South Texas: The Progressive Era*. Austin: University of Texas Press.

Andrews, David F. 1974. "A Robust Method for Multiple Linear Regression." *Technometrics 16*: 523–31.

Banfield, Edward, and Wilson, James Q. 1963. *City Politics*. New York: Vintage Books.

Baron, David P. 1993. "Government Formation and Endogenous Parties." *American Political Science Review 87*: 34–47.

Bass, Jack, and DeVries, Walter. 1976. *The Transformation of Southern Politics: Social Change and Political Consequences since 1945*. Meridian: Bloomington.

Berry, William D., and Feldman, Stanley. 1985. *Multiple Regression in Practice*. Beverly Hills, CA: Sage Foundation.

Binder, Norman E., and Garcia, Frank. 1989. "Mexican American Office Holding in Cameron County: 1876–1988." In Milo Kearney (ed.), *More Studies in Brownsville History*. Brownsville: University of Texas at Brownsville.

Black, Gordon. 1972. "A Theory of Professionalism in Politics." *American Political Science Review 68*: 865–78.

Blacksher, James U., and Menefee, Larry T. 1982. "From *Reynolds v. Sims* to *City of Mobile v. Bolden:* Have the White Suburbs Commandeered the Fifteenth Amendment?" *Hastings Law Journal 34* (September): 1–64.

Bledsoe, Timothy, and Welch, Susan. 1983. "Some Predictors of Service Representation in Urban Politics." Paper presented at the annual meeting of the American Political Science Association, Chicago.

Bridges, Edwin M., and Hallinan, Maureen. 1972. "Elected versus Appointed Board: Arguments and Evidence." *Educational Administration Quarterly 8*: 5–17.

Brieley, Allen B., and Moon, David. 1993. "Descriptive Representation and the Preception of Representation." Unpublished paper, University of Northern Iowa.

Brischetto, Robert; Cotrell, Charles L.; and Stevens, R. Michael. 1983. "Conflict and Change in the Political Culture of San Antonio in the 1970's." In David R. Johnson, John A. Booth, and Richard J. Harris (eds.), *The Politics of San Antonio: Community, Progress, Power*, pp. 75–94. Lincoln: University of Nebraska Press.

Brophy, Jere E. 1983. "Research on the Self-Fulfilling Prophecy and Teacher Expectations." *Journal of Educational Psychology 75*: 631–61.

Brown, Stephen P.; Fuchs, Beth C.; and Hoadley, John F. 1979. "Congressional Prerequisites and Vanishing Marginals: The Case of the Class of '74." Paper presented at the American Political Science Association meeting.

Browning, Rufus P.; Marshall, Dale R.; and Tabb, David H. 1984. *Protest Is Not Enough: The Struggle of Blacks and Hispanics for Equality in Urban Politics*. Berkeley: University of California Press.

Bullock, Charles S. III, and MacManus, Susan. 1990. "Structural Features of Municipalities and the Incidence of Hispanic Councilmembers." *Social Science Quarterly 71*: 665–81.

———. 1991. "Municipal Electoral Structure and the Election of Councilwomen." *Journal of Politics 53*: 75–89.

———. 1993. "Testing Assumptions of the Totality-of-Circumstances Test: An Analysis of the Impact of Structures on Black Descriptive Representation." *American Politics Quarterly 21*: 290–306.

Bullock, Charles S. III, and Stewart, Jr., Joseph. 1978. "Complaint Processing as a Strategy for Combatting Second Generation Discrimination." Paper presented at the annual meeting of the Southern Political Science Association, Altanta.

Burt-Way, Barbara J., and Kelly, Rita Mae. 1991. "Gender and Sustaining Political Ambition: A Study of Arizona Elected Officials." *Western Political Quarterly*, 11–23.

Button, James W. 1989. *Blacks and Social Change*. Princeton, NJ: Princeton University Press.

Cain, Bruce E.; Ferejohn, John A.; and Fiorina, Morris P. 1979. "What Makes Legislators in Great Britain and the United States so Popular?" Paper presented at the annual meeting of the American Political Science Association.

Campbell, Roald F.; Cunningham, Luvern L.; Nystrand, Raphael O.; and Usdan, Michael D. 1985. *The Organization and Control of American Schools*, 5th ed. Columbus, OH: Charles E. Merrill.

Carstarphen, Dana R. 1991. "The Single Transferable Vote: Achieving the Goals of Section 2 without Sacrificing the Integration Ideal." *Yale Law and Policy Review 9*: 405–29.

Cassel, Carol A. 1985. "Social Background Characteristics of Nonpartisan City Council Members: A Research Note." *Western Political Quarterly 38*: 495–501.

Cayer, N. Joseph, and Sigelman, Lee. 1980. "Minorities and Women in State and Local Government, 1973–1975." *Public Administration Review 40*: 443–50.

Chubb, John E., and Moe, Terry M. 1990. *Politics, Markets, and America's Schools*. Washington, DC: Brookings.

Cleary, Paul D., and Angel, Ronald. 1984. "The Analysis of Relationships Involving Dichotomous Dependent Variables." *Journal of Health and Social Behavior 25*: 334–48.

Clingermayer, James C., and Feiock, Richard C. 1993. "Constituencies, Campaign Support, and Council Member Intervention in City Development Policy." *Social Science Quarterly 74*: 199–215.

Cole, Richard L., and Taebel, Delbert A. 1992. "Cumulative Voting in Local Elections: Lessons from the Alamogordo Experience." *Social Science Quarterly 73*: 194–201.

Cole, Richard L.; Taebel, Delbert A.; and Engstrom, Richard. 1990. "Cumulative Voting in a Municipal Election." *Western Political Quarterly 43*: 191–99.

Crain, Robert L. 1968. *The Politics of School Desegregation*. Chicago: Aldine.

Crain, Robert L., and Street, David. 1966. "School Desegregation and School Decision-Making." *Urban Affairs Quarterly 2*: 64–82.

Davidson, Chandler, and Korbel, George. 1981. "At-Large Elections and Minority-Group Representation: A Re-examination of Historical and Contemporary Evidence." *Journal of Politics 43*: 982–1005.

De la Garza, Rodolfo O. 1984. " 'And then there were some. . . .' Chicanos as National Political Actors, 1967–1980," *Aztlan 15*: 1–24.

De la Garza, Rodolfo O., and DeSipio, Louis. 1993. "Save the Baby, Change the Bathwater, and Get a New Tub: Latino Electoral Participation after Seventeen Years of Voting Rights Act Coverage." *University of Texas Law Review 71* (June): 1479–1539.

De la Garza, Rodolfo O.; Falcon, Angelo; Garcia, F. Chris; and Garcia, John. 1992. "Ethnicity and Attitudes toward Immigration Policy: The Case of Mexicans, Puerto Ricans and Cubans in the Unted States." Paper presented at the annual meeting of the American Political Science Association, Chicago.

De la Garza, Rodolfo O.; Polinard, J. L.; Wrinkle, Robert D.; and Longoria, Tomas. 1991. "Understanding Intra-Ethnic Attitude Variations: Mexican Origin Population Views of Immigration." *Social Science Quarterly 72*: 379–87.

De la Garza, Rodolfo O., and Weaver, Janet. 1983. "Mexican Americans and Anglos in San Antonio: A City Divided." Paper presented at the annual meeting of the American Political Science Association.

De Leon, Arnoldo. 1993. *Mexican Americans in Texas: A Brief History*. Arlington Heights, IL: Harlan Davidson.

Derfner, A. 1973. "Racial Discrimination and the Right to Vote." *Vanderbilt Law Review 26*: 523.

Dickens, E. Larry. 1969. *The Political Role of Mexican Americans in South Texas.* Unpublished Ph.D. dissertation, University of North Texas.

Ducat, Craig R., and Chase, Harold W. 1988. *Constitutional Interpretation*, 4th ed. St. Paul: West.

Dutton, William H. 1975. "The Political Ambition of Local Legislators." *Polity 7*: 504–519.

Dye, Thomas R., and Renick, James. 1981. "Political Power and City Jobs: Determinants of Minority Employment." *Social Science Quarterly 62*: 475–86.

Eisinger, Peter K. 1982. "The Economic Conditions of Black Employment in Municipal Bureaucracies." *American Journal of Political Science 26*: 754–71.

Engstrom, Richard L. 1978. "Racial Vote Dilution: Supreme Court Interpretation of Section 5 of the Voting Rights Act." *Southern University Law Review 4* (Spring): 139–64.

Engstrom, Richard L., and McDonald, Michael. 1981. "The Election of Blacks to City Councils." *American Political Science Review 75*: 344–54.

———. 1982. "The Underrepresentation of Blacks on City Councils." *Journal of Politics 44*: 1088–1105.

Engstrom, Richard L., and McDonald, Michael. 1986. "The Effect of At-Large versus District Elections on Racial Representation in U.S. Municipalities." In Bernard Grofman and Arend Lijphart (eds.), *Electorial Laws and Their Political Consequences,* pp. 203–225. New York: Agathon Press.

Engstrom, Richard L.; Taebel, Delbert A.; and Cole, Richard L. 1989. "Cumulative Voting as a Remedy for Minority Vote Dilution: The Case of Alamogordo, New Mexico." *Journal of Law and Politics 5*: 469–97.

Erikson, Robert S.; Lancaster, Thomas D.; and Romero, David W. 1989. "Group Components of the Presidential Vote, 1952–1984." *Journal of Politics 51*: 337–46.

Eulau, Heinz, and Karps, Paul D. 1978. "The Puzzle of Representation: Specifying Components of Responsiveness." In Heinz Eulau and John Wahlke (eds.), *The Politics of Representation.* Beverly Hills, CA: Sage.

Finn, Jeremy D. 1982. "Patterns in Special Education Placement as revealed by the OCR Survey." In Kirby A. Heller, Wayne H. Holtzman, and Samuel Messick (eds.), *Placing Children in Special Education.* Washington, DC: National Academy Press.

Fiorina, Morris. 1977. *Congress—Keystone of the Washington Establishment.* New Haven, CT: Yale University Press.

Fowler, Linda L.; Stonecash, Jeff; and Carrothers, Robert. 1982. "It Can't Happen Here: The Incumbency Effect in State Legislatures." Paper presented at the annual meeting of the American Political Science Association, Denver.

Fraga, Luis Ricardo; Meier, Kenneth J.; and England, Robert. 1986. "Hispanic Americans and Educational Policy: Limits to Equal Access." *Journal of Politics 48*: 850–76.

Friedman, Marjorie S. 1978. *An Appraisal of the Role of the Public School as an Acculturating Agency of Mexican Americans in Texas, 1850–1968.* Unpublished Ph.D. dissertation, New York University.

Gamson, William. 1990. *The Strategy of Social Protest*, 2d ed. Belmont, CA: Wadsworth.

Garcia, F. Chris, and de la Garza, Rodolfo. 1977. *The Chicano Political Experience: Three Perspectives.* North Scituate, MA: Duxbury Press.

Garcia, F. Chris; Garcia, John A.; de la Garza, Rodolfo; and Falcon, Angelo. 1992. "The Effects of Ethnic Partisanship on Electoral Behavior: An Analysis and Comparison of Latino and Anglo Voting in the 1988 United States Presidential Election." Paper presented at the annual meeting of the American Political Science Association, Chicago.

Garcia, John A.; Garcia, F. Chris; de la Garza, Rodolfo; and Falcon, Angelo. 1992. "The Multi-Dimensionality of Ethnicity: Examining the Cases of MEXPRICUBS." Paper presented at the annual meeting of the American Political Science Association, Chicago.

Giles, Michael W., and Evans, Arthur S. 1986. "The Power Approach to Intergroup Hostility." *Journal of Conflict Resolution 30*: 469–86.

Grebler, Leo; Moore, Joan W.; and Guzman, Ralph. 1970. *The Mexican-American People.* Glencoe, IL: The Free Press.

Greene, Kenneth R. 1981. "The Impact of Electoral Competition on Service Representation by Municipal Legislators." Paper presented at the annual meeting of the Southern Political Science Association, Memphis.

Grofman, Bernard. 1982. "The Effect of Ward vs. At-Large Elections on Minority Representation." Unpublished manuscript, University of California, Irvine.

———. 1992. "Expert Witness Testimony and the Evolution of Voting Rights Case Law," pp. 197–229. In Bernard Grofman and Chandler Davidson (eds.), *Controversies in Minority Voting.* Washington, DC: Brookings.

Grofman, Bernard. 1993. Personal communication to the authors.

Grofman, Bernard. 1993b. *Minority Representation and the Quest for Voting Equality.* Cambridge: Cambridge University Press.

Guinier, Lani. 1991. "The Triumph of Tokenism: The Voting Rights Act and the Theory of Black Electoral Success." *Michigan Law Review 89* (March): 1077–1154.

Harrell, Alfreida B. Kenny. 1974. "The Voting Rights Act of 1965 and Minority Access to the Political Process." *Columbia Human Rights Law Review 6* (Spring): 129–53.

Heilig, Peggy, and Mundt, Robert J. 1984. *Your Voice at City Hall: The Politics and Policies of District Representation.* Albany: State University of New York Press.

Heller, Kirby A.; Holtzman, Wayne H.; and Messick, Samuel (eds.). 1982. *Placing Children in Special Education.* Washington, DC: National Academy Press.

Iannaccone, Laurence, and Lutz, Frank W. 1970. *Politics, Power and Policy: The Governing of Local School Districts.* Columbus, OH: Charles E. Merrill.

Jacobs, Paul W., and O'Rourke, Timothy G. 1986. "Racial Polarization in Vote Dilution Cases under Section 2 of the Voting Rights Act: The Impact of *Thornburg v. Gingles.*" *Journal of Law and Politics 3* (Fall): 295–353.

Johnson, David R.; Booth, Juhu A.; and Harris, Richard J. (eds.). 1983. *The Politics of San Antonio.* Lincoln: University of Nebraska Press.

Jones, Clinton. 1976. "The Impact of Local Election Systems on Black Political Representation." *Urban Affairs Quarterly 11*: 345–54.

Just, Anne E. 1980. "Urban School Board Elections: Changes in the Political Environment between 1950 and 1980." *Education and Urban Society 12*: 421–35.

Karlan, Pamela. 1989. "Maps and Misreadings: The Role of Geographic Compactness in Racial Vote Dilution Litigation." *Harvard Civil Rights–Civil Liberties Law Review 24* (Winter): 173–248.

Karnig, Albert K. 1976. "Black Representation on City Councils." *Urban Affairs Quarterly 12*: 2223–42.

Karnig, Albert K., and Welch, Susan. 1980. *Black Representation and Urban Policy*. Chicago: University of Chicago Press.

Karnig, Albert K.; Welch, Susan; and Eribes, Richard A. 1984. "Employment of Women by Cities in the Southwest." *Social Science Journal 21*: 41–48.

Keech, William R. 1968. *The Impact of Negro Voting*. Chicago: Rand McNally.

Keefe, Susan, and Padilla, Amado. 1987. *Chicano Ethnicity*. Albuquerque: University of New Mexico Press.

Key, V.O. 1950. *Southern Politics in State and Nation*. New York: Alfred A. Knopf.

Kosterlitz, Mary J. 1987. Note: "*Thornburg v. Gingles*: The Supreme Court's New Test for Analyzing Minority Vote Dilution." *Catholic University Law Review 36* (Winter): 531–63.

Krasker, William K. 1988. "Robust Regression." In Samuel Kotz and Norman L. Johnson (eds.), *Encyclopedia of Statistical Sciences*, vol. 8, pp. 166–69. New York: Wiley.

Leighley, Jan E. 1992. "Attitudes, Incentives and Opportunities: Group Membership and the Mobilization of Political Participation." Paper presented at the annual meeting of the Midwest Political Science Association, Chicago.

LeVarsky, Patricia A. 1987. Note: "Fair and Effective Voting Strength under Section 2 of the Voting Rights Act: The Impact of *Thornburg v. Gingles* on Minority Vote Dilution Litigation." *Wayne Law Review 34* (Fall): 303–329.

Levin, Henry M., ed. 1970. *Community Control of Schools*. Washington, DC: Brookings.

Liebert, Ronald. 1974. "Municipal Functions, Structures and Expenditures: A Reanalysis of Recent Research." *Social Science Quarterly 54*: 765–83.

Lineberry, Robert L. 1978. "Reform, Representation and Policy." *Social Science Quarterly 59*: 173–77.

Lineberry, Robert, and Fowler, Edmund. 1967. "Reformism and Public Policies in American Cities." *American Political Science Review 61*: 701–716.

Lipsky, Michael. 1980. *Street Level Bureaucracy*. New York: Russell Sage Foundation.

Lopez, Manuel M. 1981. "Patterns of Interethnic Residential Segregation in the Urban Southwest, 1960 and 1970." *Social Science Quarterly 62*: 50–63.

Loveridge, Ronald O. 1971. *City Managers in Legislative Politics*. Indianapolis: Bobbs Merrill.

Lujan, Juan R. 1976. *The Mexican American School Board Association: A Thrust toward Educational Relevancy*. Unpublished Ph.D. dissertation, University of Texas at Austin.

Lutz, Frank. 1980. "Local School Board Decision-Making: A Political-Anthropological Analysis." *Education and Urban Society 12*: 452–65.

Lyke, Robert F. 1968. "Representation and Urban School Boards." In Henry M. Levine (ed.), *Community Control of Schools*, pp. 138–68. Washington, DC: Brookings.

Lyons, W. E., and Jewell, Malcolm E. 1988. "Minority Representation and the Drawing of City Council Districts." *Urban Affairs Quarterly 23*: 432–47.

Macchiarola, Frank J., and Diaz, Joseph G. 1993. "Minority Political Empowerment in New York City: Beyond the Voting Rights Act." *Political Science Quarterly 108*: 37–57.

MacManus, Susan A. 1978. "City Council Election Procedures and Minority Representation." *Social Science Quarterly 59*: 153–61.

Manuel, Hershel T. 1930. *The Education of Spanish Speaking Children in Texas.* Austin: University of Texas Press.

Marquez, Benjamin. 1985. *Power and Politics in a Chicano Barrio: A Study of Mobilization Efforts and Community Power in El Paso.* Lanham, MD: University Press of America.

Masden, William. 1964. *The Mexican-Americans of South Texas.* New York: Holt, Rinehart and Winston.

Matthews, Donald R., and Prothro, James W. *Negroes and the New Southern Politics.* New York: Harcourt, Brace and World.

McAdams, John C. 1980. "Release Another Suspect: A Test of Fiorina's Constituency Service Hypothesis." Paper presented at the annual meeting of the Midwest Political Science Association.

McCarthy, John D., and Zald, Mayer. 1973. *The Trend of Social Movements in America.* Morristown, NJ: General Learning Press.

McCleskey, Clifton, and Merrill, Bruce. 1973. "Mexican American Political Behavior in Texas." *Social Science Quarterly 53*: 785–98.

McCleskey, Clifton, and Nimmo, Dan. 1968. "Differences between Potential, Registered and Actual Voters: The Houston Metropolitan Area in 1964." *Social Science Quarterly 49*: 103–114.

McCrone, Donald J., and Stone, Walter J. 1986. "The Structure of Consistency Representation: On Theory and Method." *Journal of Politics 48*: 956–75.

McDonald, Laughlin. 1989. "The Quiet Revolution in Minority Voting Rights." *Vanderbilt Law Review 42* (May): 1249–97.

McLemore, S. Dale, and Romo, Ricardo. 1985. "The Origin and Development of the Mexican American People." In Rodolfo de la Garza et al., eds., *The Mexican American Experience: An Interdisciplinary Anthology*, pp. 3–32. Austin: University of Texas Press.

McWilliams, Carey. 1968. *North from Mexico: The Spanish Speaking Peoples of the United States.* New York: Greenwood Press.

Meier, Kenneth J., and England, Robert E. 1984. "Black Representation and Educational Policy: Are They Related?" *American Political Science Review 78*: 392–403.

Meier, Kenneth J., and Stewart, Joseph, Jr. 1991. *The Politics of Hispanic Education.* Albany: State University of New York Press.

Meier, Kenneth J.; Stewart, Joseph, Jr.; and England, Robert E. 1989. *Race, Class and Education: The Politics of Second Generation Discrimination.* Madison: University of Wisconsin Press.

———. 1991. "The Politics of Bureaucratic Discretion: Educational Access as an Urban Service." *American Journal of Political Science 35* (February): 155–77.

Meier, Kenneth J., and Smith, Kevin B. 1993. "Politics, Bureaucracy and Minority Employment: Reexamining the Linkages." Unpublished paper, University of Wisconsin–Milwaukee.

Meier, Kenneth J., and Stewart, Joseph, Jr. 1990. "Interracial Competition in Large Urban School Districts: Elections and Public Policy." Paper presented at the annual meeting of the American Political Science Association, San Francisco.

Miller, Andrew P., and Packman, Mark A. 1987. "Amended Section 2 of the Voting Rights Act: What Is the Intent of the Results Test?" *Emory Law Journal 36* (Winter): 1–74.

Miller, Lawrence W., and Wrinkle, Robert D. 1984. "The Political Recruitment and Ambition of Local Legislators: A Southwestern Perspective." *Texas Journal of Political Studies 7*: 3–13.

Minar, David W. 1966. "The Community Basis of Conflict in School System Politics." *American Sociological Review 31*: 822–35.

Mirande, Alfredo. 1985. *The Chicano Experience: An Alternative Experience.* Notre Dame, IN: University of Notre Dame Press.

Mladenka, Kenneth R. 1989a. "Barriers to Hispanic Employment Success in 1,200 Cities." *Social Science Quarterly 70*: 391–407.

———. 1989b. "Blacks and Hispanics in Urban Politics." *American Political Science Review 83*: 165–92.

Montejano, David. 1987. *Anglos and Mexicans in the Making of Texas, 1836–1986.* Austin: University of Texas Press.

Moore, Joan, and Pachon, Harry. 1985. *Hispanics in the United States.* Englewood Cliffs, NJ: Prentice-Hall.

Morgan, David R., and Pelissero, John. 1980. "Urban Policy: Does Political Structure Matter?" *American Political Science Review 74*: 999–1006.

Morgan, David R., and Watson, Sheilah S. 1992. "Policy Leadership in Council-Manager Cities: Comparing Mayor and Manager." *Public Administration Review 52*: 438–46.

Morrison, Minion K. C. 1987. *Black Political Mobilization: Leadership, Power and Mass Behavior.* Albany: State University of New York Press.

Mosher, Frederick C. 1968. *Democracy and the Public Service.* New York: Oxford University Press.

Newman, Dianna L., and Brown, Robert D. 1992. "Patterns of School Board Decision Making: Variations in Behavior and Perceptions." *Journal of Research and Development in Education 26*: 1–6.

Note. 1982. "Alternative Voting Systems as Remedies for Unlawful At-Large Systems." *Yale Law Journal 92* (November): 144–60.

O'Connor, Karen, and Epstein, Lee. 1984. "A Legal Voice for the Chicano Community: The Activities of the Mexican American Legal Defense and Education Fund, 1968–1982." *Social Science Quarterly 65*: 245–56.

Parker, Frank R. 1990. *Black Votes Count: Political Enpowerment in Mississippi after 1965.* Chapel Hill: University of North Carolina Press.

Pelissero, John, and Morgan, David R. 1987. "State Responsiveness to School District Needs." *Social Science Quarterly 68*: 466–77.

Peterson, Paul. 1981. *City Limits.* Chicago: University of Chicago Press.

Peterson, Steven A., and Dutton, William M. 1981. "Errand Boy Behavior and Local Legislators." Paper prepared for presentation at the annual meeting of the Midwest Political Science Association, Cincinnati, April 16–18.

Pitkin, Hanna F. *The Concept of Representation.* 1967. Berkeley: University of California Press.

Polinard, J. L.; Wrinkle, Robert D.; and Longoria, Tomas. 1990. "Education and Governance: Representational Links to Second Generation Discrimination." *Western Political Quarterly, September, vol. 43:* 631–46.

———. 1991. "The Impact of District Elections on the Mexican-American Community: The Electoral Perspective." *Social Science Quarterly*

Powell, Lynda W. 1982. "Constituency Service and Electoral Margin in the Congress." Paper prepared for presentation at the annual meeting of the American Political Science Association, Denver, September 2–5.

Prewitt, Kenneth. 1970. *The Recruitment of Political Leaders: A Study of Citizen-Politicians.* Indianapolis: Bobbs-Merrill.

Rangel, Jorge, and Alcala, Carlos M. 1972. "Project Report: De Jure Segregation of Chicanos in Texas Schools." *Harvard Civil Rights–Civil Liberties Law Review 7:* 307–391.

Robinson, Theodore P., and Dye, Thomas R. 1978. "Reformism and Black Representation on City Councils." *Social Science Quarterly 59:* 133–41.

Robinson, Theodore P., and England, Robert E. 1981. "Black Representation on Central City School Boards Revisited." *Social Science Quarterly 62:* 495–502.

Robinson, Theodore P.; England, Robert E.; and Meier, Kenneth J. 1985. "Black Resources and Black School Board Representation: Does Political Structure Matter?" *Social Science Quarterly 66:* 976–82.

Rosenbaum, Robert J. 1981. *Mexicano Resistance in the Southwest: "The Sacred Right of Self-Preservation."* Austin: University of Texas Press.

Rosenbloom, David H., and Featherstonhaugh, Jeannette G. 1977. "Passive and Active Representation in the Federal Service: A Comparison of Blacks and Whites." *Social Science Quarterly 57:* 873–82.

Rubin, Donald B. 1983. "Iteratively Reweighted Least Squares." In Samuel Kotz and Norman L. Johnson (eds.), *Encyclopedia of Statistical Sciences,* vol. 8, pp. 272–75. New York: Wiley.

Samora, Julian; Bernal, Joe; and Pena, Albert. 1979. *Gunpowder Justice: A Reassessment of the Texas Rangers.* Notre Dame, IN: University of Notre Dame Press.

Sanchez, George I. 1934. *Segregation of Spanish Speaking Children in Public Schools.* Austin: University of Texas.

Sande, Milton. 1983. "Participation in Local School Board Elections: A Reappraisal." *Social Science Quarterly 64:* 647–54.

San Miguel, Guadalupe, Jr. 1979. *Endless Pursuits: The Chicano Educational Experience in Corpus Christi, Texas, 1880–1960.* Unpublished Ph.D. dissertation, Stanford University.

———. 1982. "Mexican American Organizations and the Changing Politics of School Desegregation in Texas, 1945–1980." *Social Science Quarterly 63:* 701–715.

———. 1987. *"Let Them All Take Heed": Mexican Americans and the Campaign for Educational Equality in Texas, 1910–1981.* Austin: University of Texas Press.

Schlesinger, Joseph. 1966. *Ambition and Politics.* Chicago: Rand-McNally.

Schneider, Mark. 1989. *The Competitive City*. Pittsburgh: University of Pittsburgh Press.

Seligman, Lester G. 1971. *Recruiting Political Elites*. New York: General Learning Press.

Shockley, Evelyn Elayne. 1991. Note: "Voting Rights Act Section 2: Racially Polarized Voting and the Minority Community's Representative of Choice." *Michigan Law Review 89* (February): 1038–67.

Sigelman, Lee. 1974. "State and Local Employment of Spanish-Americans in the Southwest." *Public Service 2*: 1–5.

Silver, Catherine. 1973. *Black Teachers in Urban Schools*. New York: Praeger.

Smith, Elsie, and June, Lee N. 1982. "The Role of the Counselor in Desegregated Schools." *Journal of Black Studies 13*: 227–40.

Smith, Kevin B., and Meier, Kenneth J. 1993. "Politics, Bureaucrats and Schools." Unpublished paper, University of Wisconsin–Milwaukee.

So, Alvin Y. 1987. "The Educational Aspirations of Hispanic Parents." *Educational Research Quarterly 11*: 47–53.

Soni, Sushma. 1990. "Defining the Minority-Preferred Candidate under Section 2." *Yale Law Journal 99* (May): 1651–68.

SPSS, Inc. 1988. *User's Guide*. Chicago: Spss, Inc.

Stein, Lana. 1986. "Representative Local Government: Minorities in the Municipal Workforce." *Journal of Politics 48*: 694–713.

Stein, Lana, and Condrey, Stephen. 1985. "Explication of Local Factors Affecting Minority Representation in Municipal Workforces." Paper prepared for presentation at the annual meeting of the American Political Science Association, New Orleans.

———. 1987. "Integrating Municipal Workforces: A Comparative Study of Six Southern Cities." *Publius 17*: 93–103.

Stewart, Joseph, Jr., and Sheffield, James F. 1987. "Does Interest Group Litigation Matter? The Case of Black Political Mobilization in Mississippi." *Journal of Politics 49*: 780–800.

Still, Edward. 1984. "Alternatives to Single Member Districts." In Chandler Davidson (ed.), *Minority Vote Dilution*, pp. 249–70. Washington, DC: Howard University Press.

———. 1992. "Cumulative and Limited Voting in Alabama." In Wilma Rule and Joseph F. Zimmerman (eds.), *United States Electoral Systems: Their Impact on Women and Minorities*, pp. 183–96. New York: Praeger.

Stimson, James A. 1985. "Regression in Space and Time: A Statistical Essay." *American Journal of Political Science 29*: 914–47.

Stinson, Rodney. 1993. "Your Money Is Being Buried in the Not-the-Taj-Mahal." *San Antonio Express-News*, January 23: A–2.

Stone, Clarence N. 1989. *Regime Politics: Governing Atlanta, 1946–1988*. Lawrence: University Press of Kansas.

Stone, Clarence N., and Sanders, Heywood T. (eds.). 1987. *The Politics of Urban Development*. Lawrence: University of Kansas Press.

Stone, Walter J. 1979. "Measuring Constituency-Representative Linkages: Problems and Prospects." *Legislative Studies Quarterly 4*: 623–41.

Strike, Kenneth A. 1993. "Professionalism, Democracy and Discursive Communities: Normative Reflections on Restructuring." *American Educational Research Journal 30*: 255–75.

Svara, James H. 1991. *A Survey of America's City Councils: Continuity and Change.* Washington, DC: National League of Cities.

Taebel, Delbert A. 1977. "Politics of School Board Elections." *Urban Education 12*: 153–66.

———. 1978. "Minority Representation on City Councils: The Impact of Structure on Hispanics and Blacks." *Social Science Quarterly 59*: 142–52.

Thernstrom, Abigail M. 1987. *Whose Votes Count? Affirmative Action and Minority Voting Rights.* Cambridge, MA: Harvard University Press.

Thomas, Sue. 1992. "The Effects of Race and Gender on Constituency Service." *Western Political Quarterly, March, vol. 45*: 169–80.

Thompson, Joel A., and Moncrief, Gary F. 1993. "The Implications of Term Limits for Women and Minorities: Some Evidence from the States." *Social Science Quarterly 74*: 310–21.

Tucker, Harvey J., and Zeigler, L. Harmon. 1977. "Responsiveness in Local Politics: A Comparative Analysis of Local School Boards." Paper prepared for presentation at the annual meeting of the Western Political Science Association, Phoenix.

Tufte, Edward R. 1974. *Data Analysis for Politics and Policy.* Englewood Cliffs, NJ: Prentice-Hall.

Tyack, David B. 1974. *The One Best System: A History of American Urban Education.* Cambridge, MA: Harvard University Press.

Vedlitz, Arnold, and Johnson, Charles A. 1982. "Racial Segregation, Electoral Structure and Minority Representation." *Social Science Quarterly 63*: 729–36.

Villarreal, Roberto E. 1979. *Chicano Elites and Non-Elites: An Inquiry into Social and Political Change.* Palo Alto, CA: R & E Research Associates.

Vogel, Ronald K. 1992. *Urban Political Economy.* Gainesville: University Press of Florida.

Wainscott, Stephen H., and Woodard, J. David. 1988. "Second Thoughts About Second-Generation Discrimination." *American Politics Quarterly 16*: 171–92.

Weinberg, Meyer. 1977. *A Chance to Learn: The History of Race and Education in America.* Cambridge: Cambridge University Press.

Welch, Susan. 1990. "The Impact of At-Large Elections on the Representation of Blacks and Hispanics." *Journal of Politics 52*: 1050–76.

Welch, Susan, and Bledsoe, Timothy. 1988. *Urban Reform and Its Consequences: A Study in Representation.* Chicago: University of Chicago Press.

Welch, Susan, and Karnig, Albert. 1979. "Correlates of Female Office Holding in City Politics." *Journal of Politics 41*: 478–91.

Welch, Susan, and Sigelman, Lee. 1993. "The Politics of Hispanic-Americans: Insights from National Surveys, 1980–1988." *Social Science Quarterly 74*: 76–94.

Wolfinger, Raymond E. 1965. "The Development and Persistence of Ethnic Voting." *American Political Science Review 59*: 896–908.

Wolfinger, Raymond E., and Field, John O. 1966. "Political Ethos and the Structure of City Government." *American Political Science Review 60*: 306–326.

Wrinkle, Robert D., and Miller, Lawrence. 1984. "Errand Boy or Constituency

Service: A Multi-State Study of Municipal Legislators." Unpublished paper, University of Texas–Pan American.

Yiannakis, Diana. 1981. "The Grateful Electorate: Casework and Congressional Elections." *American Journal of Political Science 25*: 568–80.

Zax, Jeffrey S. 1990. "Election Methods, Black and Hispanic City Council Membership." *Social Science Quarterly 71*: 339–55.

Zeigler, Harmon; Kehoe, Ellen; and Reisman, Hane. 1985. *City Managers and School Superintendents: Responses to Community Conflict.* New York: Praeger.

Zeigler, L. Harmon; Jennings, M. Kent; with Peak, G. Wayne. 1974. *Governing American Schools: Political Interaction in Local School Districts.* North Scituate, MA: Duxbury Press.

Index

About the Authors

J. L. Polinard is a Professor in the Department of Political Science at the University of Texas–Pan American. His research interests are in the areas of public law and minority politics. He has published in *Publius, Social Science Quarterly, Social Science Journal, State and Local Government Review,* and *Western Political Quarterly.*

Robert D. Wrinkle is a Professor at the University of Texas–Pan American, where he teaches in the Master of Public Administration program. Among his teaching and research interests are public policy and urban politics. He is the editor of *Politics in the Urban Southwest* and has published in *State and Local Government Review, Urban Law Review, Western Political Quarterly, Social Science Journal,* and *Social Science Quarterly.*

Tomas Longoria is an Assistant Professor in the Department of Political Science at the University of Wisconsin–Milwaukee. His primary interests are in urban policy and urban politics. He has published in *Urban Affairs Quarterly, State and Local Government Review, Western Political Quarterly, Social Science Journal,* and *Social Science Quarterly.*

Norman E. Binder is a Professor of Political Science at the University of Texas at Brownsville. His research interests include minority and ethnic politics as well as Latin American politics. He is the author of a study of Mexican American office holding in south Texas.

For Product Safety Concerns and Information please contact our EU
representative GPSR@taylorandfrancis.com
Taylor & Francis Verlag GmbH, Kaufingerstraße 24, 80331 München, Germany

www.ingramcontent.com/pod-product-compliance
Lightning Source LLC
Chambersburg PA
CBHW050437280326
41932CB00013BA/2152

* 9 7 8 1 5 6 3 2 4 3 4 9 3 *